Richard Brinsley Sheridan

Sean Elliott

GREENWICH EXCHANGE
LONDON

Greenwich Exchange, London

Richard Brinsley Sheridan
© Sean Elliott 2014

First published in Great Britain in 2015
All rights reserved

Printed and bound by **imprint**digital.net
Typesetting and layout by Jude Keen Ltd., London
Tel: 020 8355 4541

Cover image: © Mary Evans Picture Library

Greenwich Exchange Website: www.greenex.co.uk

Cataloguing in Publication Data is available
from the British Library.

ISBN: 978-1-906075-91-0

for Brendan

Contents

Chronology

1671 George Villiers, *The Rehearsal*.

1697 John Vanbrugh, *The Provoked Wife*.

1700 William Congreve, *The Way of the World*.

1704 Colley Cibber, *The Careless Husband*.

1722 Richard Steele, *The Conscious Lovers*.

1728 John Gay, *The Beggar's Opera*.

1737 Robert Walpole's Licensing Act re-establishes Covent Garden and Drury Lane as the only two patented theatres in London.

1747 9 April, David Garrick becomes co-patentee of Drury Lane Theatre.

1749 Birth of Johann Wolfgang von Goethe.

1751 Birth of Richard Brinsley Sheridan in Dublin.

1755 Publication of Samuel Johnson's *Dictionary*.

1758 The Sheridan family moves to England.

1759 Birth of Friedrich Schiller.

1761 Birth of August von Kotzebue.

1766 22 September, Sheridan's mother, Frances, dies.

1769 Garrick organises the Shakespeare Jubilee at Stratford. Founding of the *Town and Country Magazine* mentioned by name in *The School for Scandal*.

1772 Founding of *The Morning Post*, notorious for printing scandal.

1773 Oliver Goldsmith, *She Stoops to Conquer*. 6 September, Sheridan marries Elizabeth Linley.

1774 Death of Goldsmith. Goethe's novel *The Sorrows of Young Werther* becomes an international bestseller.

1775 17 January, *The Rivals* first performed at The Theatre Royal, Covent Garden. 21 November, *The Duenna* performed at Covent Garden. Beginning of the American War of Independence.

1776 10 June, Garrick's farewell performance at Drury Lane.

1777   24 February, premiere of *A Trip to Scarborough* at Drury Lane. 8 May, *The School for Scandal* first performed at Drury Lane.

1779   20 January, death of Garrick. 30 October, first performance of *The Critic* at Drury Lane.

1780   Drury Lane damaged in the Gordon Riots.

1781   Friedrich Schiller, *The Robbers.*

1782   Sarah Siddons establishes her reputation as a major tragic actress at Drury Lane.

1783   John Philip Kemble joins Drury Lane.

1788   Beginning of the trial of Warren Hastings. Kemble becomes manager of Drury Lane. 14 August, Thomas Sheridan dies.

1789   Beginning of the French Revolution; Sheridan makes speeches in Parliament in support of it but Edmund Burke and many other Whigs oppose the revolution.

1791   Drury Lane closes.

1792   28 June, Elizabeth Sheridan dies.

1793   21 January, execution of Louis XVI.

1794   28 July, execution of Maximilien Robespierre. The rebuilt Drury Lane opens.

1795   Sheridan marries Hester Jane Ogle.

1798   The Irish Rebellion. July, Napoleon invades Egypt. Elizabeth Inchbald's *Lovers' Vows*, adapted from a play by August von Kotzebue, is a success at Covent Garden.

1799   24 May, *Pizarro* performed at Drury Lane.

1801   Union of Great Britain and Ireland.

1803   Kemble and Siddons leave Drury Lane to perform at Covent Garden.

1804   Napoleon plans to invade England.

1805   Death of Schiller.

1807   Slave trade is abolished in the British Empire.

1808   Covent Garden burns down. Publication of Goethe's *Faust, Part One.*

1809   24 February, Drury Lane Theatre burns down. Sheridan is financially ruined.

1812   Siddons retires. 12 October, the rebuilt Drury Lane Theatre opens.

1814   Edmund Kean makes his debut at Drury Lane.

1816   7 July, death of Sheridan.

1

Sheridan's Life and Background

There is an ambiguity to Richard Brinsley Sheridan's character; his enemies called it hypocrisy. His Victorian biographer, Margaret Oliphant, complained that 'He is like two men, one of them painfully building up what the other every day delights to pull down.' The many images of him seem to be of two different men. There is the slim young man of the 1770s, who eloped with his first wife, fought two duels with her persecutor and wrote three of the wittiest comedies of the eighteenth century. Then there is the fat Whig politician depicted in the satirical cartoons of his later years who, like many of his aristocratic friends, squandered money, pursued women and drank heavily.

Sheridan's whole career was marked by this ambiguity. Both his energy and his laziness became legendary. He worked hard to achieve theatrical and political eminence but he also displayed a comic ingenuity in avoiding the responsibilities that came with his position. His plays have autobiographical elements but they also derive much from the stock characters and situations of Restoration Comedy. He claimed that politics had no place in the theatre and with his last play, *Pizarro*, wrote a work full of lengthy speeches about liberty and the evils of colonialism. As a politician, he was both a close friend of George IV and a champion of the French Revolution.

Sheridan's doubleness began with his birth in Dublin in 1751. He never denied his Irish heritage but sought the political power that was only available to an English gentleman. Some other Dubliners who rose to eminence in the eighteenth century rigorously denied any suggestion that they might be Irish. The dramatist Richard Steele described himself as 'an Englishman born in the city of Dublin', while the Duke of Wellington joked that being born in a stable did not turn a man into a horse. Sheridan left Ireland at the age of eight never to return. In his biography of Sheridan, *A Traitor's Kiss* (1997), Fintan O'Toole sees the playwright's Irish origin as the key to his identity:

'Sheridan looks contradictory because he lived in two places – a real England and a passionately imagined Ireland – at the same time.'

Sheridan's family background had its own ambiguities. As a playwright, he inherited an enviable legacy. He was the son of Ireland's foremost actor, Thomas Sheridan, who managed the Smock Alley Theatre in Dublin during the late 1740s and early 1750s. Thomas' interest in the stage was derived from his passion for the spoken word. In his *A Discourse being Introductory to his course of Lectures on Elocution and the English Language* (1759) Thomas argued for 'the vast superiority' of spoken over written language because the speaker's appearance gives us valuable clues about his or her sincerity: 'whilst the charmed ear easily admits the words of truth, the faithful eye, even of the illiterate, can read their credentials in the legible hand of Nature, visibly characterised in the countenance and gesture of the speaker.' Sheridan had a difficult relationship with Thomas who regarded his elder son, Charles, as the more promising of the two boys. The authoritarian father in *The Rivals*, Sir Anthony Absolute ('I am compliance itself – when I am not thwarted') was probably inspired by Thomas. If this is so, Sheridan sweetened the portrait; after his son's secret marriage to Elizabeth Linley, it took years before Thomas would again acknowledge his existence.

Sheridan's mother, Frances, was a playwright and a novelist. She was admired by the famous novelist Samuel Richardson and by David Garrick, who staged her *The Discovery* at Drury Lane in 1775 in competition with her son's play *The Rivals* at Covent Garden. Her wit had an acerbic quality, she dismissed both her sons in a letter as 'impenetrable dunces'.

Sheridan's poor academic record as a schoolboy confirmed his mother's low opinion of his intelligence. When his parents left England for France to escape their debts, he remained at Harrow. Sheridan's sense of desertion had lasting psychological effects. Throughout his life he remained afraid of the dark and he became morbidly protective of the health of his own children. Frances' death before Sheridan turned fifteen probably compounded his feelings about the vulnerability of those he loved. Although he attended an elite public school, his social status was dubious. He was sneered at by the other pupils as 'the actor's son'. In eighteenth-century England family connections were important in defining a person's identity. Paradoxically, his family's eminent position in the theatre proved a disadvantage in a society which saw actors as little more than prostitutes and vagabonds. When Sheridan became a politician, his opponents led by William Pitt the younger sought to discredit him by suggesting that as a man of the theatre he was hardly a gentleman and should return to his 'proper sphere'.

In 1770 the Sheridan family moved to Bath and Thomas summoned his son to join them. Over the previous decade, Bath had been transformed from a backwater inhabited by invalids drinking its curative waters into an important meeting place for the social elite. Those wishing to join that elite or profit from them were drawn to the expanding city. Given the importance of genteel behaviour and of correct pronunciation in this new community, Thomas attempted to gain a reputation by giving elocution lessons. He joined with Thomas Linley in arranging evenings of music and literary readings to publicise his abilities. Linley's family were all talented musicians. Linley's son Tom struck up a friendship with Mozart while studying in Florence and later wrote music for Sheridan's comic opera *The Duenna*. After Tom's tragic death in a boating accident in 1778 at the age of twenty-two, Mozart spoke of him as a man who 'would have been one of the greatest ornaments of the musical world.'

Sheridan's most important relationship, however, was with Tom's sister Elizabeth Linley. Elizabeth was already a famous singer. Her concerts commanded packed houses, Thomas Gainsborough painted her repeatedly and Sir Joshua Reynolds portrayed her as Saint Cecilia, the patron saint of music. As a celebrity, Elizabeth's love life became the subject of gossip. Her engagement to a rich and much older man had been mysteriously broken off, a story which inspired Samuel Foote's play *The Maid of Bath* (1771). She was also courted by a married man, Captain Mathews, with whom she exchanged letters. Sheridan intervened; he eloped with Elizabeth, was married to her in France by a Catholic priest and fought two duels with Mathews. The second duel left Sheridan badly wounded. A year later, in 1773, he married Elizabeth in a Protestant ceremony.

This romantic adventure gained the young couple a lot of press attention. While recovering from his second duel, Sheridan read the papers and joked: 'Let me see what they report of me today, I wish to know whether I am dead or alive.' He gained a reputation as a chivalrous gentleman and a fearless duellist with a famous wife. The truth was less heroic. His second duel with Mathews was a brutal struggle in which the two men rolled on the ground while stabbing at each other with broken swords. It is possible that Elizabeth and

Mathews were having an affair (as Mathews later claimed) and that Sheridan, after becoming her confidant, outmanoeuvred his married rival.

After their marriage Sheridan declared that his wife would no longer sing in public. Samuel Johnson praised this decision; in his view it proved that Sheridan was not an adventurer, prepared to live off his wife's earnings, but a man of principle. Restricting access to Elizabeth was, however, also a shrewd move. Those wealthy and influential people who wanted to hear her sing had to invite her as a guest, rather than as a hired performer, to their homes and so were also obliged to invite her husband. In this way, he gained access to Devonshire House, where the Duchess of Devonshire acted as the hostess for the Whig faction of Parliament. Amanda Foreman's biography *Georgiana, Duchess of Devonshire* (1998) gives a typically paradoxical depiction of Sheridan as a member of the Devonshire House Circle: 'The playwright and arch-scrounger Richard Brinsley Sheridan was one of its stars. An incorrigible drinker, womanizer and plotter, he embodied the best and worst of the Circle. He was brilliant yet lazy, kind-hearted yet remiss over honouring his debts to the point of dishonesty.'

Sheridan had no career and no income but plenty of charm. He talked Thomas Harris, the manager of Covent Garden, into staging *The Rivals* and then quickly wrote it. The play was first staged on 17 January 1775 and was a flop. Elizabeth wrote to Sheridan assuring him of her love but declaring that he was certainly not a playwright. He revised his play and persuaded Covent Garden to stage it again ten days later. This time it was a triumphant success. In his Preface to the published text, Sheridan attributed the initial failure of *The Rivals* to 'the uncommon length of the piece on the first night', to the poor performances of several of the actors and – ironically considering that Sheridan had been born in Dublin – to his depiction of Sir Lucius O'Trigger, regarded by the reviewers as offensive to Irishmen. Sheridan accepted an audience's reaction as an important part of the creative process: 'I see no reason why the Author of a Play should not regard a First Night's Audience as a candid and judicious friend attending in behalf of the Public at his last Rehearsal.' From this point onwards, he carefully gauged the audience's response to his work and would rewrite passages which failed in performance.

Sheridan followed his first theatrical success with an even greater one at the end of the same year. Enlisting the assistance of his father-in-law and his brother-in-law, he wrote a comic opera for Covent Garden. Although it is now little known, *The Duenna* (1775) was an unprecedented popular hit, running for over seventy consecutive nights. On the strength of *The Duenna* the literary world started to notice Sheridan; Samuel Johnson recommended the young playwright for membership of the prestigious Literary Club because 'He who has written the two best comedies of his age, is surely a considerable man.' Sheridan's reception at Devonshire House became warmer and he was introduced to the charismatic leader of the Whig party, Charles James Fox. Fox was a heavy drinker, a compulsive gambler and, despite his ugliness, a notorious womaniser. Sheridan soon adopted Fox's aristocratic habits.

Since 1660 London had only had two licensed theatres, Covent Garden and Drury Lane. The repressive Licensing Act of 1737 (effectively a form of state censorship) reinforced the monopoly of the two theatres. As the rising star of Covent Garden, Sheridan caught the attention of David Garrick, the ageing actor manager of Drury Lane. During the 1740s Garrick's transformation from an unsuccessful wine merchant into a famous actor was as miraculous as Sheridan's rise in the 1770s. The French philosopher Denis Diderot in his *The Paradox of the Actor* (written 1770 to 1784) claimed that anyone wanting a true artistic education would learn as much from seeing Garrick act as from visiting the antiquities of Rome. Garrick became the manager of Drury Lane in 1747. His marriage to Eva Maria Veigel in 1749 was an intense artistic partnership. There is a perceptive portrait of the young couple by William Hogarth. Garrick is seated and working at his desk, he looks up with amusement as his wife grabs at his quill pen over his shoulder. The Garricks laugh together but only as an interruption to hard and dedicated work. Garrick championed the educational value of the theatre. His portrayals of Macbeth and Richard III were instrumental in increasing Shakespeare's reputation. His organisation of the first Shakespeare Jubilee held in Stratford in 1769 is sometimes derided because none of Shakespeare's works were performed but it offered a symbolically important moment.

Garrick knew Sheridan's parents. He performed in Dublin in 1745 at Thomas Sheridan's invitation and admired Frances' plays. By 1775, he wanted to retire as the manager of Drury Lane. He encouraged Sheridan to buy him out and, with two partners, the young playwright accomplished this ambition in 1776. Garrick soon regretted his decision. In a letter of 17 July 1777 to the actor Tom King he lamented 'Poor old Drury! It will be, I fear, very soon in the hands of the Philistines.' Sheridan did not share Garrick's canonical beliefs and the two men were temperamental opposites. Sheridan ridicules the idea that drama has an educational function in *The Critic*, he refers to Shakespeare in all three of his major comedies but did not admire Shakespeare's plays and, instead of dedicating himself to the theatre, he used the profits from Drury Lane to finance his political career.

Sheridan began at Drury Lane by staging some of the late Restoration plays (written in the 1690s), which were important models for his own work. In accordance with the genteel taste of his times he toned down the sexual references in his light revisions of three of William Congreve's plays. He also substantially recast John Vanbrugh's *The Relapse* (1696) into *A Trip to Scarborough* (1777). Sheridan was not prudish, however; like the Restoration authors, he enjoyed scandalous stories. After leaving Harrow he had collaborated with his school friend Nathaniel Halhed on an unperformed play based on the myth of Amphitryon but set in modern times, in which the god Jupiter commits adultery with Amphitryon's wife to conceive Hercules. Sheridan and Halhed then published a poetry collection loosely translated from a late Greek author, *The Love Epistles of Aristanetus* (1771), which included such poems as 'A panegyric on a dainty courtesan' and 'The Expedient' concerning 'an ingenious device practised by a lady of gallantry to deceive a suspicious husband'. The original version of *The Rivals* included a risqué remark by Sir Anthony Adverse about a cucumber. With the beginning of the eighteenth century, however, public opinion increasingly discouraged the explicit treatment of extra-marital relationships on the stage. Colley Cibber's *The Careless Husband* (1704) offers an early example of this coyness. The heroine, Lady Easy, discovers her husband in post-coital slumber with their maid but the lovers are both dressed and sitting in separate chairs; the only indication that adultery has occurred is that the husband has removed his wig. Sexual behaviour could only be staged in a codified way. Sheridan admitted that his censored versions of Congreve's plays were inferior to the originals: 'they are like horses, when you deprive them of their vice, they lose their vigour … ' Despite Sheridan's reputation among his contemporaries as the 'modern Congreve', these muted productions disappointed his audience.

Sheridan silenced his critics with *The School for Scandal* (1777), which became the most frequently performed play in the last quarter of the eighteenth century and has never lost its popularity. Although the play borrowed from Restoration authors, it was seen as a comic depiction of the Devonshire House Circle with Georgiana as the model for Lady Teazle. Consequently *The School for Scandal* managed to be both old fashioned in its dramatic technique and daringly contemporary. Sheridan refused to have it published and obsessively revised the play. The actor manager Sir Johnston Forbes-Robertson in his autobiography, *A Player Under Three Reigns* (1925) recalls meeting a woman in Bayreuth whose husband was 'the direct descendant of Richard Brinsley Sheridan. Some years after at her beautiful home in England, she showed me the original manuscript of "The School for Scandal", every page of which was so scored with emendations, transpositions, and altering of sentences that I came by the familiar lines at some trouble.'

In 1779 Sheridan wrote his last comedy, *The Critic*, a burlesque piece about the nature of the theatre and theatrical illusion. His evasiveness and laziness were becoming legendary. Two days before *The Critic* was to be performed it was still unfinished. In desperation Tom King, the actor playing Puff, lured Sheridan to the Drury Lane green room which contained two bottles of claret, some anchovy sandwiches and some writing materials. King locked Sheridan in and explained that he would not be leaving until the play was finished. Sheridan polished off the play, the sandwiches and the wine.

Linda Kelly in her biography of Sheridan marvels at the eminence he achieved before turning thirty: 'He was the most successful playwright of the age. Young, charming, with a wife whose fame matched his own, he was lionised in the drawing-rooms of London.' But this was also a turning point in Sheridan's life. He had written his best plays. In 1780 he became a Member of Parliament for Stafford and he spent the next decade building his reputation as a political orator. His place in the Devonshire House circle caused him to distance himself from his wife while he pursued titled women. Elizabeth followed his example and had an affair with Lord Edward Fitzgerald, the Irish revolutionary, resulting in the birth of a daughter in 1792. Elizabeth, whose health had never been good, died shortly afterwards. Sheridan remarried in 1795. His second wife, Hester Jane Ogle, was nineteen and he was forty-three.

It is difficult to assess how much information to give about Sheridan's political career in a book which focuses on his literary achievement. Some critics assert that his politics are implicit in everything he wrote and must not be ignored, others disagree and claim that his comedies are essentially apolitical. Arnold Hare's *Richard Brinsley Sheridan* (1981) argues that, whatever Sheridan's wishes, it would have been impossible for him to stage overtly political material:

> A young man setting out to write successful theatrical comedy in the 1770s had certain matters to take into account. The censorship meant that he had to avoid political affairs, and since the Lord Chamberlain's office was manned by members of the Establishment of the day, he had to keep clear also of social attitudes that were too revolutionary, or that offended prevailing standards of taste in middle- and upper-class circles. Otherwise, performances would simply not have been allowed.

Near the end of his life Sheridan warned his business partner, Samuel Whitbread, in a letter of 7 March 1815 to 'Keep politics out of the Theatre'. But Sheridan did not follow his own advice. The political statements in his plays became more overt as his career progressed. *The Rivals* considers the education for women, *The School for Scandal* contains some social criticism and explores media manipulation and *The Critic* extends the theme of media manipulation while mocking the government's disastrous handling of the American Wars. Finally, the late tragedy *Pizarro* (1799) carries an emotive anti-colonial message.

Linda Kelly asserts that 'Viewed politically, Sheridan's career can be regarded as a splendid failure.' Certainly Sheridan spent most of his political career in opposition and had little direct impact on the governing of Britain. More recent critics, notably Fintan O'Toole and David Francis Taylor, insist on his importance as a voice of dissent. He consistently favoured the cause of liberty and self-determination. He regarded the American Revolution with sympathy and supported Catholic emancipation in Ireland. In the 1780s he made his reputation as an orator through his speeches urging the impeachment of Warren Hastings. The trial was not simply about whether Hastings had committed criminal acts in India (he was eventually acquitted), it concerned the ethics of British interference in the governing of India and the rise of Imperialism. This issue caused widespread public unease. The hero of Henry Mackenzie's *The Man of Feeling* (1771), one of the novels Lydia Languish is reading in *The Rivals*, uttered his own protest:

> You tell me of immense territories subject to the English: I cannot think of their possessions, without being led to enquire, by what right they possess them. They came there as traders, bartering the commodities they brought for others which their purchasers could spare; and however great their profits were, they were equitable. But what title have the subjects of another kingdom to establish an empire in India?

In 1789 the French Revolution divided the Whig party, ending all hope that it might be elected. Fox and Sheridan saw the Revolution as the dawn of a new age but Edmund Burke, along with many other Whigs, was appalled by the bloodshed and the collapse of social order.

Given his support of the American and French Revolutions, Sheridan's relationship with the British royal family was understandably strained. George III favoured the Tories rather than the Whigs who sought to curb the power of the monarchy. The Hanovers, however, were so unpopular in England that even the Tories found them an embarrassment. Walter Savage Landor's 'The Four Georges' expressed the widespread detestation:

> George the First was always reckoned
> Vile, but viler George the Second
> And what mortal ever heard
> Any good of George the Third,
> But when from earth the Fourth descended
> God be praised the Georges ended.

George III is probably the author of an anonymous satirical attack, written in 1784, on Sheridan's character and his talent for social climbing. The Prince of Wales, the future George IV, in opposition to his father, allied himself with the Whigs and befriended Sheridan. There was a hopeful period in the 1780s when the easy-going Prince seemed to promise the Whigs a future in government. Sheridan encouraged Parliament to pay off the Prince's massive debts at a time when British subjects were dying of poverty. Sheridan played a critical role in advising the Prince during the constitutional crisis caused by George III's madness and persuaded the Prince to keep his marriage to a Catholic widow, Mrs Fitzherbert, secret.

Sheridan's parallel career as the manager of Drury Lane lurched between disaster and absurdity. He ran up substantial debts and actors complained about his slowness in paying their wages. He was accused of valuing profitability over artistic merit. He banked on the 'rediscovered' Shakespearean tragedy *Vortigern* (1796) causing enough controversy to make money, even though the play was a poor forgery. In this case he miscalculated and the play closed after a single disastrous performance. He had better luck with a performing dog called Carlos who appeared in *The Caravan, or, The Driver and his Dog* (1803) and nightly saved a child from drowning. The dog proved a box-office success and won Sheridan's affection.

Despite his unreliability, Sheridan revealed a talent at Drury Lane for recruiting gifted people. In 1778 he briefly employed his touchy but perceptive father as the acting manager. Thomas recognised Sarah Siddons' potential and helped to train her into the most powerful tragic actress of her generation. Her performances were so overwhelming that other actors sometimes burst into tears while sharing the stage with her. In 1783 Sarah's brother John Philip Kemble joined the company and soon began to act as Sheridan's artistic director. Like Garrick and unlike Sheridan, Kemble and Siddons loved Shakespeare. Kemble played Hamlet as a Renaissance superman, an ideal humanist paralysed by his own greatness; he was also an outstanding Coriolanus, using his production to protest against the anarchy of the French Revolution. Siddons was a compelling Lady Macbeth and made an important contribution to the Romantic Movement's understanding of Shakespeare through her psychological reading of the part. William Hazlitt called her 'tragedy personified'.

Sheridan was admired by several key figures in the rising Romantic Movement. The anarchist philosopher and novelist William Godwin, the father of Mary Shelley, was a journalistic ally in the 1780s. Samuel Taylor Coleridge published a sonnet in Sheridan's praise in the *Morning Chronicle* on 14 January 1795. According to Coleridge's son, Derwent, the poet's play *Remorse* (1797) 'was written expressly for the stage, at the instigation, and with the encouragement of Mr Sheridan, by whom, however, it was not deemed suitable for that purpose. Ultimately it was brought out at Drury Lane Theatre in the year 1813, under the auspices of Lord Byron and Mr Whitbread, when it ran for twenty nights'. Just as Sheridan wrote a dramatic poem for Drury Lane on the death of Garrick, Byron wrote the 'Monody on the Death of the Right Hon. R.

B. Sheridan, Spoken at Drury Lane Theatre', which calls Sheridan 'Of human feelings the unbounded lord' and claims that as an orator he was 'the delegated voice of God!'

Apart from his later plays, Sheridan's greatest impact on Drury Lane was his decision, after the theatre's closure in 1791, to rebuild it with a much larger auditorium. Sheridan followed the trend towards expansion that both Drury Lane and Covent Garden had pursued throughout the eighteenth century to entertain an ever-growing London population. The new Drury Lane, which reopened in 1794, encouraged an exaggerated style of acting involving gestures that could be seen at a distance, and plays which favoured dramatic spectacle over subtlety. The age of the melodrama was dawning.

Sheridan's last play, *Pizarro*, based on a text by the German dramatist August von Kotzebue, made full use of the recently rebuilt and expanded Drury Lane's technical resources to include a battle among the mountains between a group of exaggeratedly noble Peruvians and the Spanish Conquistadors. *Pizarro* was condemned by the critics but, as Kelly notes, its popular success 'was phenomenal. It ran for thirty-one nights (excluding Sundays) in succession, an unprecedented run for a tragedy. Thirty thousand copies of the play were sold, and thousands of people who had never thought of the matter before plunged deep into Peruvian history.'

After 1800 Sheridan's career began to decline. In 1802 Kemble and Siddons left Drury Lane for Covent Garden. In 1806 the death of Fox deprived Sheridan of his closest political ally. Sheridan's drinking, gambling and womanising undermined his health and his second marriage. On 24 February 1809 Drury Lane burnt down, leaving him bankrupt. This disaster led to a celebrated anecdote:

> Sheridan sat drinking with his friends in the Piazza Coffee House watching the destruction of his property with stoic fortitude. One of them remarked on his calm and Sheridan, witty even in calamity, made his famous reply: 'A man may surely be allowed to take a glass of wine beside his own fireside.'

Such comic anecdotes about Sheridan's last years have a bittersweet taste. When a fellow guest at a dinner party asked him what kind of wine he liked best, Sheridan replied 'Other people's.' The comment is amusing but it suggests a man forced to live off the generosity of others. In October 1812 he lost his seat in Parliament and consequently his immunity from prosecution for debt. He endured poverty and was imprisoned at least once. In 1813, there is a glimpse of him at another dinner party praising Jane Austen's *Pride and Prejudice* and telling the lady next to him 'to buy it immediately for it was one of the cleverest things he had ever read.' He died on Sunday 7 July 1816, in a house that had been emptied of its possessions by the bailiffs. His wife died a year later from cancer of the womb.

Sheridan's funeral in Westminster Abbey was as splendid as his last days had been squalid. His coffin bearers included the Bishop of London, three earls, a duke and a lord. Recalling Sheridan's impoverished death, Thomas Moore described the event with indignation:

> O it sickens the heart to see bosoms so hollow,
>   And friendships so false in the great and high-born; –
> To think what a long line of titles may follow
>   The relics of him who lay friendless and lorn!

Moore's biography, the *Memoirs of the Life of the Right Honourable Richard Brinsley Sheridan* (1825) remains a major source for material about Sheridan's literary career. It includes early drafts of passages from the best-known plays and lengthy extracts from his unfinished works. Moore had a lot to recommend him as a biographer. He had known Sheridan and he had the cooperation of Sheridan's younger son Charles. As a famous poet and song-writer Moore possessed literary talent and, as a Dublin-born Irishman who joined the Whig intelligentsia, he followed a similar career path to Sheridan. The preface to the anonymous *Sheridaniana* (1826), however, insists that Moore had failed to evoke Sheridan's character: 'throughout the work, Mr Moore seems to be far more anxious to prove that *he* can say fine things, than to show that Sheridan was in the habit of saying them. The *Sheridaniana* are intended to supply this deficiency in Mr Moore's work.' The *Sheridaniana* is a collection of chiefly comic anecdotes arranged in a roughly chronological order. These anecdotes depict Sheridan as good hearted, heavy drinking and always witty. Not all of the anecdotes are biographically accurate. Sheridan became the kind of semi-mythical personage who attracts good stories.

Victorian biographies wrestled with this exaggerated legend. Oliphant's *Sheridan* (1883), for instance, interprets Sheridan's life as an example of what happens to those who frivolously waste their talents: 'There came a moment when everybody with one accord ceased and even refused to be amused by these eccentricities any longer, and found them to be stale jests, insolences, and characterised by a selfish disregard of everybody's comfort but his own.' Few recent critics would adopt Oliphant's rhetoric but the assertion that Sheridan failed to fulfil his potential occasionally resurfaces. The legend surrounding him resembles the one that surrounds the film director Orson Welles. A slim and handsome young genius, who rules the artistic world at thirty, degenerates into an obese, prevaricating charmer. The early promise is frittered away in unfinished projects and endless talk. The creator of memorable drama dwindles into the subject of other people's anecdotes. The fact that this is the 'stuff of legends' should encourage us to distrust it.

Perhaps because of the oppressive censorship of the period, none of the eighteenth-century dramatists combines quality with productivity. There were plenty of prolific but mediocre dramatists (such as Richard Cumberland whom Sheridan satirised as Sir Fretful Plagiary in *The Critic*) and there were several important writers such as John Gay and Oliver Goldsmith who wrote one or two excellent plays. Ironically, by the standards of his time, Sheridan *was* prolific – who else between the death of George Farquhar in 1707 and the rise of Oscar Wilde and George Bernard Shaw in the 1890s, wrote so many enduring plays? Additionally, both Wilde and Shaw owe Sheridan considerable stylistic debts. Shaw who had been a music critic, and so did not make musical analogies lightly, claims that 'Sheridan wrote for the actor as Handel wrote for a singer'. The theatre critic Michael Billington notes of the late eighteenth-century British drama that 'It was, in many ways, a dying theatre: and Sheridan brought it new life.' But Sheridan did more than revivify the theatre of his day. In our own age of increasingly diverse social media his witty exploration of the terrain where news blurs into gossip has gained a new importance.

2

The Rivals

For many critics, Sheridan's first play is his best. Although *The Rivals* had a hostile reception on its first performance at Covent Garden on 19 January 1775, the revised version staged on the 28th of the same month instantly became a favourite with audiences and the play has a long performance history. By 1778 it had also been staged in America and Germany.

Its appeal is easy to recognise: *The Rivals* offers larger-than-life comic characters, absurd situations and some harmless fun. For its early audiences, its blamelessness was one of its major recommendations. Most of the characters are well meaning and no one is entirely malevolent. The elder characters, Sir Anthony Absolute and Mrs Malaprop, who fill the traditional role of blocking agents opposed to the marriage of the young lovers, only offer a token resistance. Equally, Jack Absolute's two rivals for Lydia's love are never a creditable threat. The quarrelsome Sir Lucius O'Trigger is deceived by Lucy into believing that Lydia welcomes his love letters, which she never receives, while Bob Acres is a stereotypical country bumpkin. Mrs Malaprop, as Lydia's guardian, insists in Act One that she is 'under no positive engagement to Mr Acres' and is happy to accept Jack as Lydia's suitor.

The Rivals offers the familiar comedic structure in which two contrasting pairs of lovers (a witty couple, Jack and Lydia, who provide comic banter and a second, more serious couple, Faulkland and Julia, who embody deeper feelings) overcome the objections to their eventual marriages. Consequently the play has some resemblance to other popular English comedies involving a quartet of lovers, including Shakespeare's *Much Ado About Nothing*, George Etherege's *The Man of Mode* and George Farquhar's *The Beaux' Stratagem,* but Sheridan daringly provides his lovers with almost no external obstacles to their desires. He even reverses the audience's expectations by having Sir Anthony and Mrs Malaprop encourage

Jack and Lydia to marry. Tiffany Stern in her introduction to the second New Mermaid edition (2004) of the play questions the apparent thinness of Sheridan's material: 'What can be the structure of a play in which so little happens?'

The Rivals is equally 'harmless' in its lack of overt sexual material. Sheridan owed a substantial literary debt to the Restoration playwright William Congreve. Sir Anthony Absolute resembles the headstrong Sir Sampson Legend in Love for Love (1695). Mrs Malaprop recalls Lady Wishfort in The Way of the World (1700), who also believes that she is carrying on a courtship with an Irish peer. Both of these older women regard themselves as desirable but are described harshly by male characters, Mrs Malaprop as an 'old weather-beaten she-dragon' and Lady Wishfort as an 'antidote to lust'. Sheridan differs from Congreve in his indirect approach to sex. His sister Alicia on his return from Harrow was struck by his 'innocuous wit, that was shown afterwards in his writings'. It is partly because of this 'innocuous wit' that Sheridan remained popular throughout the nineteenth century when critics such as Thomas Babington Macaulay condemned Restoration Comedy for its immorality. But Lydia's suggestively titled library books and Faulkland's nightmarish monologues provide The Rivals with a troubling vision of sexuality.

Lydia and Faulkland, rather than an external cause, offer the only serious obstacles to the marriages of the four lovers. Lydia opposes the financial view of marriage favoured by Mrs Malaprop and Sir Anthony, which sees a good match as the mutually beneficial union of two family fortunes. Lydia and Sir Anthony view the bride as little more than an animal to be purchased. In Act Five Lydia complains that after all her romantic dreams of elopement she will be turned into 'a Smithfield bargain' (Smithfield was London's meat market). Sir Anthony explains to his son that a wife is simply the 'livestock' that comes with an estate:

Absolute: [Y]ou talked to me of independence and a fortune, but not a word of a wife.
Sir Anthony: Why what difference does that make? Od's life, sir! If you have the estate, you must take the livestock on it, as it stands.

Sheridan's irony concerning the differing views about marriage in the play is pervasive. Sir Anthony is mocked for regarding a wife as livestock; Mrs Malaprop develops the argument that financial prosperity is more important than love to the point where she claims that ''tis safest in matrimony to begin with a little *aversion*'. Conversely Lydia's determination to sacrifice her fortune unnecessarily for the sake of love is inspired by her reading of romances ('But you know I lose most of my fortune if I marry without my aunt's consent till of age; and that is what I have determined to do, ever since I knew the penalty'). The 'sensible' Julia Melville and Jack Absolute are subject to irony because of the lengths they go to for their imaginative partners. Julia agrees to flee the country after Faulkland persuades her that he is a murderer. The wealthy Jack creates a second identity – and so becomes his own rival – as Ensign Beverley to fulfil Lydia's fantasy of a poor but noble suitor. There is a comic vignette of Jack's sufferings as Beverley in Lydia's description of their romantic, and uncomfortable, meetings:

> How often have I stole forth, in the coldest night in January, and found him in the garden, stuck like a dripping statue! There would he kneel to me in the snow, and sneeze and cough so pathetically! He shivering with cold and I with apprehension! And while the freezing blast numbed our joints, how warmly would he press me to pity his flame, and glow with mutual ardour!

Lydia's account of these passionate trysts is a good example of Sheridan's comic strategy of undercutting romance with practical details. Lydia is so carried away by the romantic situation she has arranged that she transforms unromantic details such as coughing and sneezing into part of her fantasy. There is a collision between the literal and metaphorical: the 'flame' of love burns intensely but it cannot warm up a garden on the 'coldest night in January'. Lydia is not, however, merely a target for Sheridan's irony, her insistence on the importance of love and her passion for reading have their serious aspects.

During her first appearance, in Act One, Scene 2, Lydia is associated with twenty books. For an audience hearing these titles briefly rattled off in the theatre, the books evoke an impression of her sentimental interests (*The Man of Feeling, The Tears of Sensibility* and *A Sentimental Journey*) and her enjoyment of sexually suggestive material (*The Mistakes of the Heart, The Delicate Distress*). This reading matter touches on continuing cultural anxieties about what young women know about sex and where they get their information.

The books mentioned were all popular works. A salacious title like *The Innocent Adultery* was even used for several different texts. Sheridan may be referring to Thomas Southerne's play about bigamy *The Fatal Marriage, or, The Innocent Adultery* (1694) or to the anonymous novel *Harriet, or, The Innocent Adulteress* (1771) but the most likely possibility is Paul Scarron's novella *The Innocent Adultery* (1691). Scarron's story involves a heroine, Eugenia, who is married to Don Sancho, a much older man. During the first half of the tale, she tries unsuccessfully to have an affair with Andrada, a young courtier; she is eventually raped by her brother-in-law and stabs him to death in vengeance. Her husband dies of grief and, after a period of repentance, she marries a man of her own age. In closing Scarron assures the reader that 'our bridegroom convinced Eugenia the first night of his bedding her, that he was another sort of a man than Don Sancho, and she found in him what she had not found in the Portuguese Andrada.' Lydia is reading about sexual transgression and about what kind of men make the best lovers. Henry Mackenzie's *The Man of Feeling* (1771) involves a warning about what might happen to women with romantic illusions. In Mackenzie's novel, Emily Atkins, like Lydia, is inspired by 'those poetical descriptions of the beauty of virtue and honour, which the circulating libraries easily afforded'; she is seduced by her lover, follows him to London and is placed by him in a brothel. Lydia's reading emphasises her naivety but it allows her to encounter questions about women and desire. Outside of her fantasies about Beverley, Lydia can be surprisingly unromantic. When Julia admits that she loves Faulkland because he saved her from drowning, Lydia is unimpressed: 'Why a water-spaniel would have done as much! Well, I should never think of giving my heart to a man because he could swim!'

The subplot between Julia and Faulkland parallels the conflict between Jack and Lydia but with a reversal of roles: Julia is sensible while Faulkland strives for an idealised love. Although this subplot was popular in the eighteenth century and Sheridan liked Faulkland enough to extend his speeches in subsequent productions, by the nineteenth century this second romance was often edited out of performances. Linda Kelly argues that the subplot belongs to a particular cultural moment: 'Julia and Faulkland present us with the greatest difficulty because they belong so much to a period that had an intense admiration for delicacy of mind and sensitivity of feeling.' She adds that 'Faulkland's feverish questioning of Julia's love, and the sentimental rhetoric he employs, are hard to put across today'.

Sheridan wrote *The Rivals* when the cult of sentimentality was sweeping across Europe. The movement prioritised spontaneous feeling over thought. It asserted that the whole of humanity irrespective of race, gender, nationality or age was united by benevolent impulses. One of the greatest virtues that a person could possess was compassion for the suffering of others. Public displays of emotion were seen as creditable and men who cried were particularly praiseworthy. In his minor classic about the period, *The Age of Scandal* (1950), T.H. White has a chapter entitled 'Tears', which mentions Sheridan's tendency to weep openly; it also notes that:

> We have a fashion in the twentieth century of considering tears to be unmanly, so we assume that they have always been effeminate. But there have been periods when it has been correct for males to cry, and when males have cried, loud and long, about a surprising variety of subjects, to the applause and even to the admiration of their friends.

Eighteenth-century sentimental writers extolled the wisdom of the heart. Jean-Jacques Rousseau's *Émile* (1762) argued for an educational system that favoured a return to nature over rote learning. William Wordsworth, in book XII of *The Prelude* (1805), expressed a key concern of any 'Man of Feeling' when he lamented over:

> The differences, the outside marks by which
> Society has parted man from man,
> Neglectful of the universal heart.

Sheridan is sometimes associated with Oliver Goldsmith as part of an 'anti-sentimental' movement. Goldsmith's 'An Essay on the Theatre, or a Comparison between Laughing and Sentimental Comedy' (1773) deplores 'the weeping sentimental comedy so much in fashion at present' and calls for the return of 'true comedy' which excites laughter by 'rendering folly or vice ridiculous'. Goldsmith warns that if playwrights continue to blur the distinction between tragedy and comedy then an important comic tradition will vanish: 'It is not easy to recover an art when once lost; and it will be but a just punishment, that when, by our being too fastidious, we have banished humour from the stage, we should ourselves be deprived of the art of laughing.'

Sheridan inherited Goldsmith's legacy in some quite immediate ways. Five of the important roles in *The Rivals* were taken by actors who had appeared in the first production of Goldsmith's *She Stoops to Conquer* (1773). Goldsmith died in 1774 but his influence would still have been strong in January 1775. Although his attitude towards sentimental comedy is more ambivalent than Goldsmith's, Sheridan's best plays treat the cult of sentimentality with some irony. In *The School for Scandal*, Joseph's hypocrisy takes the form of pretending to deep feelings that he does not possess (he is 'a sentimental knave'). In *The Critic*, the platitudes of sentimental tragedy, including the plight of young lovers divided by the fate of nations, are parodied. In *The Rivals*, the sentimental Lydia and Faulkland are exposed as self-indulgent characters. Their 'sensibility' is a form of egotism. Faulkland proudly refuses to hide his unhappiness – instead he parades his misery and spoils the mood of his companions:

> **Faulkland**: Why, Jack, have I been the joy and spirit of the company?
> **Absolute**: No, indeed you have not.
> **Faulkland**: Have I been lively and entertaining?
> **Absolute**: O, upon my word, I acquit you.
> **Faulkland**: Have I been full of wit and humour?
> **Absolute**: No, faith. To do you justice, you have been confoundedly stupid indeed.

Faulkland's indignant catechism is ironic. Instead of proving that he is a man of integrity, he demonstrates how annoying he can be. A more mature man would not have drawn attention to his unhappiness. Julia helps Faulkland to gain this emotional maturity. J.B. Priestley in his *Particular Pleasures* (1975) recalls Claude Rains in the role in a 1925 production of *The Rivals* at the Lyric Hammersmith Theatre. Priestley praises Rains for giving Faulkland an intellectual complexity and briefly indicates the problems with the part: 'As a rule this neurotically jealous character is played as if he were rather a bore, clearly part of a sub-plot, but in this particular production, with Rains playing him, he dominated the piece.' Faulkland represents an aspect of Sheridan's character. Cecil Price argues that 'Sheridan's own temperament was an uneasy mixture of the satirical and the sentimental: he laughed at Faulkland but also luxuriated in his fevered sensibility.' Michael Billington goes further, claiming that the character gives the play its energy:

I believe, however, there is something more than Sheridan's comic inventiveness that keeps the play alive; and that is his penetrating observation of a certain kind of manic-depressive, self-torturing lover in the relatively minor character of Faulkland. Someone once defined love as 'egoisme à deux', and Faulkland is a perfect example of that as he throws himself into agonies of mad jealousy and needless distrust, wild optimism and black despair. Successive actors, from Paul Daneman to Tom Courtenay to James Aubrey, have made the Faulkland-crisis the emotional pivot of the play; which only goes to prove that romantic self-infatuation is as prominent today as it was two hundred years ago.

Act One of *The Rivals* is dominated by the monologues of three women (Julia, Mrs Malaprop and Lucy) and all three of these speeches concern correct social behaviour. Mrs Malaprop outlines her views on women's education, Lucy closes the act with her argument that servants should pretend to be less intelligent than they really are and Julia, in the first long speech of the play, defends Faulkland from Lydia's charge that he is jealous, selfish and inconsiderate:

> No, Lydia, he is too proud, too noble, to be jealous; if he is captious, 'tis without dissembling; if fretful, without rudeness. Unused to the fopperies of love, he is negligent of the little duties expected from a lover – but, being unhackneyed in the passion, his affection is ardent and sincere, and, as it engrosses his whole soul, he expects every thought and emotion of his mistress to move in unison with his. Yet, though his pride calls for this full return, his humility makes him undervalue those qualities in him which would entitle him to it; and not feeling why he should be loved to the degree he wishes, he still suspects that he is not loved enough. This temper, I must own, has cost me many unhappy hours, but I have learned to think myself his debtor for those imperfections which arise from the ardour of his attachment.

Goldsmith's 'An Essay on the Theatre' associates the rise of sentimental comedy with the rise of the modern novel in the eighteenth century: 'Those abilities that can hammer out a novel are fully sufficient for the production of sentimental comedy.' Julia's character analysis of Faulkland is arguably more typical of the novel than of a theatrical monologue. She asserts that his problems are psychological ones: his apparent pride is based on a crippling lack of self-worth. He does not believe that anyone could love him and so he expects to be betrayed. Faulkland comically suggests his sexual unease when he objects to Julia dancing with other men: 'there never can be but *one* man in the world, whom a truly modest and delicate woman ought to pair with in a country-dance; and even then, the rest of the couples should be her great uncles and aunts!' His sexuality becomes more pathological in Act Three when he imagines himself 'punished' for his ill-treatment of Julia by being forced to marry and have sex with an old crone: 'may I lose her forever, and be linked instead to some antique virago, whose gnawing passions and long-hoarded spleen shall make me curse my folly half the day and all the night!' This nightmare possibly contains a death-wish; the 'antique virago' with her 'gnawing passions' becomes Faulkland's own suicidal impulses. His yearning for an absolute passion ('he expects every thought and emotion of his mistress to move in unison with his') is the tragic equivalent to Lydia's snowbound garden (acceptable for a brief romantic fantasy but ultimately life-threatening).

The Rivals was staged less than a year after the publication of Johann Wolfgang Goethe's internationally bestselling novel *The Sorrows of Young Werther* (1774), in which the brilliant but unstable Werther is consumed by love for Charlotte and commits suicide. (Goethe acknowledges his indebtedness to contemporary English literature when Werther and Charlotte enthusiastically discuss Goldsmith together.) Despite the differences between a tragic novel and a comedy of manners, there is a resemblance between Werther, the suicide, and Faulkland, who repeatedly tries to destroy his own happiness. Neither character has to face an external enemy. Although both are intelligent and articulate men, they prioritise feeling over intellect and so intensify their struggles against their own violent emotions. Werther is angry when he is valued by a sympathetic nobleman for his scholarly gifts rather than for his passionate heart; Faulkland judges Julia's actions according to whether they show emotional depth. Unfortunately, strong feelings can have trivial causes. Faulkland is heartbroken because Julia appeared happy at a dance, Werther commits suicide because he believes that a happily married woman whom he hardly knows should have been his soul mate. Werther dies because he cannot cope with his feelings. Faulkland survives because he learns to subdue his emotions to a recognised social code represented by Julia. Otherwise he would become the outcast possessed by 'gloomy and unsocial fits' that he imagines when he tests her by claiming that he has committed murder. His homicidal lie contains a psychological truth.

The setting of *The Rivals*, the city of Bath, reflects the uncertainty that many of the characters feel about 'correct' social conduct. When the Sheridan family arrived in Bath in September 1770 the city had a paradoxical air. Its Roman ruins testified to its antiquity but the place had recently become fashionable and was going through a building boom. The iconic Royal Crescent was completed in 1775. Robert Southey (who was born in nearby Bristol) emphasises Bath's fascinating modernity in his *Letters from England* (1807): 'If other cities are interesting as being old, Bath is not less so being new. It has no aqueduct, no palaces, no gates, castle, or city walls, yet it is the finest and most striking town that I have ever seen.' For Sheridan and his generation Bath as a 'new' and expanding city, which attracted a dazzling but mixed society, was a disorientating place. It threw people together who would normally never have met. This led to questions of correct behaviour in large gatherings. Beau Nash became the first of a series of unofficial Masters of Ceremony with the final word on questions of etiquette. The first scene of *The Rivals* concerns the conversation of two servants and briefly outlines Fag's view of how to behave in Bath:

> In the morning we go to the Pump Room, though neither my master nor I drink the waters. After breakfast we saunter on the Parades or play a game at billiards. At night we dance, but – damn the place – I'm tired of it! Their regular hours stupefy me: not a fiddle nor a card after eleven!

Sir Lucius O'Trigger, Bob Acres and Sir Anthony Absolute all come to Bath on questions of matrimony. Bob and Sir Lucius believe they are courting Lydia, while Sir Anthony wants to arrange a marriage with Lydia on his son's behalf. This is in keeping with the city's reputation as a good place to make a match (Jane Austen's heroine in *Northanger Abbey* will later find a husband there) but all three men fail to fit in with the prevailing social code. Sir Lucius arranges a duel in a city where the carrying of swords is forbidden. He is fooled by Lucy into exchanging love letters with Mrs Malaprop instead of Lydia (Mrs Malaprop's use of the poetic pseudonym Delia makes this deception easier) and his courtship of the wrong woman highlights his ineptitude. In the first version of the play, Sir Lucius finally agrees to marry Mrs Malaprop for the sake of her money but it is perhaps more appropriate that he remains an outsider. Bob Acres attempts to fit in by overdressing and cultivating what Jack calls a 'new method of swearing'; these attempts only emphasise his position as a country bumpkin or 'eccentric planet' on an outer orbit around the fashionable world. Sir Anthony Absolute, in contrast to his son who cultivates two separate identities, can only be his unchanging self in any situation. He is 'absolute' in his determination to have his 'own way' and consequently does not belong in a city of civilised compromises.

As a headstrong character who can only be herself, Mrs Malaprop resembles Sir Anthony. For generations of theatre-goers, however, she has remained a unique figure and one of the chief attractions of the play. Frances Sheridan created a character with an equally wayward vocabulary in her unfinished play, *A Journey to Bath*; Sheridan used some of his mother's malapropisms, including the reference to the 'contagious countries'. These linguistic mistakes have a long comic tradition. Shakespeare's Dogberry from *Much Ado About Nothing*, the Mechanicals in *A Midsummer Night's Dream* and Mistress Quickly in *Henry V* all confuse similar-sounding words. Such errors suggest that the character concerned has aspirations beyond his or her present position and so attempts to speak in an elevated way. Significantly, Mrs Malaprop's first long speech is about female education. She wishes to be admired for her erudition and also wants other women to have greater educational opportunities. Sheridan had argued in an early, unpublished essay for a higher standard of education for women. Consequently, despite making considerable comic capital from this monologue, he gives Mrs Malaprop a certain dignity:

Observe me, Sir Anthony. I would by no means wish a daughter of mine to be a progeny of learning; I don't think so much learning becomes a young woman; for instance – I would never let her meddle with Greek, or Hebrew, or Algebra, or Simony, or Fluxions, or Paradoxes, or such inflammatory branches of learning – neither would it be necessary for her to handle any of your mathematical, astronomical, diabolical instruments. But, Sir Anthony, I would send her, at nine years old, to a boarding-school, in order to learn a little ingenuity and artifice. Then, Sir, she should have a supercilious knowledge in accounts; and as she grew up, I would have her instructed in geometry, that she might know something of the contagious countries; but above all, Sir Anthony, she should be mistress of orthodoxy, that she might reprehend the true meaning of what she is saying. This, Sir Anthony, is what I would have a woman know; and I don't think there is a superstitious article in it.

Like Lydia and Faulkland, Mrs Malaprop is unaware of the ironic aspect of her own remarks. Her wish that her hypothetical daughter might know 'the true meaning of what she is saying' is poignant considering Mrs Malaprop's own linguistic problems but her verbal confusions also challenge the audience's knowledge of language. Some of her errors are easy to spot ('reprehend' for 'apprehend', for instance). Other errors cause a slight hesitation and may even reveal a concealed meaning. By the 'contagious countries' Mrs Malaprop means the 'contiguous countries' but 'contagious' slyly evokes an insular British attitude (if you go abroad you will only catch something nasty). The confusion of 'superficial' and 'supercilious' in 'a supercilious knowledge' suggests how people behave superciliously when their superficial knowledge of a subject leads them to claim an authority or expertise they do not possess. Occasionally Mrs Malaprop's vocabulary puzzles the scholars: is she using the wrong word or the right one? Her claim that young girls should learn 'a little ingenuity and artifice' is perhaps correct (or more truthful than she realises); women need to learn duplicity, 'ingenuity and artifice', to survive in a man's world, especially in the patriarchal society of eighteenth-century England. It is doubtful, though, that she would openly admit this to the chauvinistic Sir Anthony. Mrs Malaprop is a great comic creation but the audience's laughter is tinged with unease. Everyone, no matter how well educated, has mispronounced a word or mistaken its meaning at some point. Many of us have humiliating memories of our linguistic errors and there is always the possibility of a similar humiliation in the near future. Many of Mrs Malaprop's errors involve a theological vocabulary: 'simony' (the buying or selling of religious offices), 'diabolical', 'orthodoxy' and 'superstitious'. Mrs Malaprop's fondness for theological words has an imaginative truth. Every time we speak we make a leap of faith in our belief that we will be understood. Potentially, we are all Mrs Malaprop.

At the heart of *The Rivals* is Jack Absolute's courtship of Lydia. Unlike the characters that surround him, Jack lacks eccentricities. He may be derived from the gallants of Restoration comedy but he is not a libertine. From the beginning of the play his love for Lydia is a given and there is no hint of any interest in other women. His assumed identity as Ensign Beverley suggests an element of deviousness and his reluctance to marry Lydia without her fortune (which he could do at any time) conveys his practicality. Like many of Sheridan's lovers, he knows the importance of money but he is also prepared to defy his father for the woman he loves. Despite his dual identity, he does not go through a change of personality like Faulkland or a change of heart like Lydia; he is the same person at the end of the play as at the beginning. His steadfastness highlights Sheridan's technical ingenuity in structuring his play. William Hazlitt particularly admired Sheridan's art in balancing the two parallel scenes between Jack and his father. In Act Two, Jack defies his father's wish to marry him to an unknown bride and in Act Three, Scene 1 Jack, after learning that this bride is Lydia, becomes a comic paragon of submission to his father's will. His most significant moment occurs before the play begins when, as Ensign Beverley, he waits in a freezing garden in January to meet Lydia. The assignation is an absurd one but Jack chooses to fulfil Lydia's fantasy. Sheridan warns against the dangers of confusing fantasy with reality (of throwing away a real fortune, as Lydia intends, to inhabit a make-believe world of loving poverty) but he also recognises the importance of the imagination. Lydia is right: love means keeping your appointment in a snowbound garden.

3

St Patrick's Day, The Duenna and *A Trip to Scarborough*

The three plays discussed in this chapter are rarely revived today and often only briefly discussed in studies of Sheridan's work. All three have merit and offer new perspectives on Sheridan's major comedies but their neglect is understandable. The short *St Patrick's Day* was dashed off in forty-eight hours as a vehicle for Lawrence Clinch, the actor who took over the role of Sir Lucius O'Trigger in *The Rivals* after the first, unsuccessful performance. Like most farces it is as Cecil Price notes 'far more entertaining when seen than when read.' *The Duenna: A Comic Opera* is witty and contains some attractive characters but seems thin on the page, especially since its plot is stereotypical and involves little conflict. *A Trip to Scarborough* is a more substantial play but it is also a censored reworking of John Vanbrugh's Restoration Comedy *The Relapse* (1696).

These three plays, however, span an important period in Sheridan's life. *St Patrick's Day* and *The Duenna* were written and performed at Covent Garden in 1775, the same year as *The Rivals*. *The Duenna* both consolidated Sheridan's reputation and increased it. Linda Kelly notes that '*The Rivals* had made Sheridan's name as a playwright, but *The Duenna* was a still greater success. It ran for seventy-five days in its first season, ten days longer than *The Beggar's Opera* had done nearly half a century earlier.' After this phenomenal hit it became impossible for anyone working in the theatre to ignore the twenty-four-year-old playwright. Most importantly, it impressed David Garrick, the manager of London's other patent theatre, Drury Lane. Garrick wanted to retire and Sheridan was suddenly a plausible successor. In September 1776 Sheridan headed a partnership which bought Garrick out and became the principal manager of Drury Lane, a position he held for over thirty years. He opened his first season at the theatre with the revival of three plays by William

Congreve, a major influence on his own comedies. Unfortunately the public response was mixed. *A Trip to Scarborough* was Sheridan's attempt to disarm his critics by providing a comparatively original work, while also proclaiming his debt to Restoration Comedy. Its depiction of the rivalry of two brothers for one woman and its cautious treatment of adultery, foreshadows the plot of *The School for Scandal*, the play that would give Sheridan artistic authority at Drury Lane.

St Patrick's Day is a short work which includes some of Sheridan's favourite comic strategies in a simplified form. The 'Scheming Lieutenant' of the play's subtitle is the wily Irish Lieutenant O'Connor who wants to marry Lauretta. The match is opposed by her father, Justice Credulous. With the help of the melancholy widower, Doctor Rosy, O'Connor disguises himself as 'Honest Humphrey', and defeats several soldiers singlehandedly in a rehearsed fight. The watching Credulous is deceived and hires Humphrey as a bodyguard to keep the soldiers away from his daughter. Credulous soon catches 'Humphrey' kissing Lauretta and orders him out of the house. O'Connor writes to Credulous claiming that he poisoned the Justice's morning cup of chocolate. Living up to his name, Credulous believes O'Connor's note; Doctor Rosy introduces a 'German Quack' who 'has antidotes for all poisons'. Credulous' wife, Bridget, enthusiastically urges her husband to die out of principle rather than owe his life to a disreputable person. Credulous however agrees to let the Quack marry Lauretta if he will provide a cure. Once this promise is in writing the Quack removes his disguise and reveals that he is O'Connor and that Credulous was not poisoned.

As with *The Rivals*, *St Patrick's Day* gains a lot of its humour from opposing high-minded romanticism to cynical pragmatism. Bridget's exhortation to her husband not to fear death provides an example:

> **Justice**: I will not die, Bridget – I do not like death.
> **Bridget**: Pshaw! there's nothing in it – a moment and it is over.
> **Justice**: Ay, but it leaves a numbness behind, that lasts for a plaguy long time.

Bridget is as fascinated with the magic power of words as Mrs Malaprop in *The Rivals*. She complains that her daughter would have been obedient if she had been given a Biblical name but 'Lauretta' is an incitement to bad behaviour, it is 'a runaway name.' Lauretta recalls

Lydia Languish in her blend of romantic fantasy and surprising brutality. Her fantasies about officers ('the prettiest men in the World') combine sexuality with death: 'give me the bold, upright, noble Youth, – who makes love one day, and has his head shot off the next – ' Bridget's reply that she would not want a husband who left one leg in Boston when the rest of him returns to London is a reminder of the ongoing American war that Sheridan returns to in *The Critic*.

St Patrick's Day breaks new ground for Sheridan. Doctor Rosy, who in recalling his dead wife Dolly, sententiously moralises on the brevity of life, prefigures Joseph Surface's moral sentiments in *The School for Scandal*. O'Connor's dislike of overdone make-up ('there is nothing on Earth so impudent as an everlasting blush') anticipates the unkind exchanges about ladies who use cosmetics clumsily in the same play. In *St Patrick's Day*, Sheridan repeatedly experiments with dialogue in which the conversationalists ignore each other and continue with their different subjects. The encounter between Doctor Rosy, who meditates on the vanity of wealth and status in the face of mortality, and O'Connor, who has just been thrown out of Credulous' house, resembles a duet in a musical:

> **Lieutenant:** O Doctor! Ruined and undone!
> **Doctor:** The Pride of Beauty –
> **Lieutenant:** I'm discovered, and –
> **Doctor:** The gaudy Palace –
> **Lieutenant:** The Justice is –
> **Doctor:** The pompous wig –
> **Lieutenant:** More enrag'd than ever.
> **Doctor:** The gilded Cane –
> **Lieutenant:** Why, Doctor.
> **Doctor:** Hey!

As Fintan O'Toole argues, the play provides a 'positive and defiant image of Irish nationality'. While consenting to O'Connor's marriage to his daughter Credulous makes his own demands:

> **Justice:** You're an Irishman, and an officer, ar'n't you?
> **Lieutenant:** I am, and proud of both.
> **Justice:** The two things in the world I hate most – So mark me – Forswear your Country, and quit the Army – and I'll receive you as my Son in law.

O'Connor indignantly refuses on both counts and still wins Lauretta. Curiously, in a play entitled *St Patrick's Day* (Ireland's national day) it is sometimes difficult to identify which characters are Irish. Although Flint is an English name, Corporal Flint is probably an Irish character because he served for 'three years within a little bit' with O'Connor in the Royal Inniskillins, an Irish regiment. Bridget's name is Irish and might hint that his troubled marriage is the reason for Credulous' antipathy to Ireland. The play lightheartedly captures the paradoxes and confusions of Anglo Irish identity in the 1770s. The marriage of O'Connor and Lauretta, in which both retain their cultural identities, optimistically envisions an equal partnership between the two nations.

The creation of *The Duenna* demonstrated Sheridan's ability to utilise the talents of other people. His marriage to the singer Elizabeth Linley encouraged him to write a comic opera. He recruited her father Thomas Linley to write music and to set Sheridan's lyrics to traditional Irish and Scots tunes. Equally, Elizabeth's brother, Tom, composed over half the original music. As Michael Cordner notes 'The original manuscript of the libretto is in Elizabeth's handwriting, and it seems likely that Sheridan, lacking musical training, leaned greatly on her advice.'

The exceptional success of *The Duenna*, which opened at Covent Garden on 21 November 1775, gained Sheridan the attention of the literary world. Samuel Johnson invited him to join the prestigious Literary Club, where his fellow members included David Garrick. It is possible that Sheridan wrote a Spanish Comedy to gain Garrick's attention. One of the actor's favourite parts was Don Felix in another Spanish Comedy, Susannah Centlivre's *The Wonder* (1714), the role Garrick would play in his farewell performance. The genre of Spanish Comedies gained popularity with Sir Samuel Tuke's *The Adventures of Five Hours* (1662), an adaptation of a Spanish play once attributed to Calderon. The Spanish stereotypically had a repressive attitude towards women; in Tuke's play Don Carlos speaks of 'that Severity to Women,/Which grows to be a National reproach/Unto us all abroad'. The title of Sheridan's musical hints at this severity; a *duenna* is an older woman employed by a wealthy family to ensure an unmarried woman's chastity by acting as her inseparable companion. In contrast to the Comedy of Manners genre, Spanish Comedies were characterised by swordplay and vigorous action. Heroines were often about to enter a nunnery or marry a man chosen by their authoritarian fathers. Additionally, these heroines usually had a jealous brother and had to flee their homes in disguise before finding true love. These plays were not always set in Spain. The best known of them today, Aphra Behn's *The Rover* (1777), is set in the Spanish-occupied Italian city of Naples. It was enough that they should be 'Spanish' in atmosphere and involve questions of honour.

The plot of *The Duenna* resembles that of Centlivre's *The Wonder* in focusing on a quartet of lovers, including one heroine who is on the eve of an arranged marriage, while the second heroine is under compulsion to become a nun so that her inheritance may be claimed by other members of her family. Don Jerome has determined that his daughter, Louisa, will marry Isaac Mendoza, a rich Portuguese Jew. She is in love with Antonio and exchanges places with her ugly Duenna, Margaret, to escape her father's home. (The two women wear veils to achieve this deception.) The Duenna pretends to be Louisa and persuades Isaac to elope with her. Louisa's brother Ferdinand is in love with Clara, whose father and 'unnatural stepmother' (neither of whom appear on stage) want her to become a nun on the next day. Clara also runs away from home and seeks refuge in the convent of Saint Catherine. Louisa pretends to be Clara, which misleads Ferdinand into believing that Antonio is pursuing the woman he loves. In the third act, the lovers meet at the convent and the misunderstandings are resolved. They are married at the nearby friary while Isaac is tricked into marrying the Duenna. Jerome is consoled for his daughter's marriage to the penniless Antonio by Ferdinand's marriage to an heiress.

The play is remarkable for its lack of substantial complications. The schemes of the respective lovers succeed at the first attempt. The misunderstanding between Ferdinand and Antonio over Clara does not lead to a duel and the villains of the piece, Jerome and Isaac, are scarcely punished. Jerome acquires more money through his son's marriage. Although Isaac storms off the stage (like Malvolio in *Twelfth Night*) after discovering that he has been duped, he has previously admitted that he finds ugly women more approachable than beautiful ones: 'Nothing keeps me in such awe as perfect beauty. Now there is something consoling and encouraging in ugliness.' Margaret follows him and it is possible that they will be happy together.

Given the play's lack of conflict and its stereotypical characters, it must have won over its early audiences by its charm. William Hazlitt claims in his *Lectures on the English Comic Writers* (1819) that '*The*

Duenna is a perfect work of art. It has the utmost sweetness and point.' Its popularity finally dwindled in the 1840s. Nigel Playfair staged *The Duenna* in 1924 at the Lyric, Hammersmith in London to good reviews; several beautiful costume designs and paintings of the production are housed at the Victoria and Albert Museum, including one of Playfair as Don Jerome. Generally, though, the play has suffered from theatrical and critical neglect. In *Sheridan and the Drama of Georgian England* (1976), John Loftis dismisses *The Duenna* as 'a museum piece, in which serious comments on human affairs have little part.' It gained a kind of afterlife when the composer Sergei Prokofiev based his *Betrothal in a Monastery* (1940) on his own Russian translation of Sheridan's libretto.

When the English Touring Opera revived *The Duenna* in 2010, Michael Billington suggested in the *Guardian* ('The Duenna's 230-year Elopement', 29 September 2010) that the play's neglect is due to the anti-Semitic portrayal of Isaac. The director of the ETO production, Michael Barker-Caven denied the accusation: 'Sheridan's criticism of Isaac is not that he's a Jew, but that he has turned his back on his real identity.' In Act One, Scene 2, Louisa and Ferdinand try to persuade Don Jerome that Isaac would not make a suitable husband:

> **Jerome**: And pray, what is your objection to him?
> **Ferdinand**: He is a Portuguese in the first place.
> **Jerome**: No such thing, boy; he has forsworn his country.
> **Louisa**: He is a Jew.
> **Jerome**: Another mistake: he has been a Christian these six weeks.
> **Ferdinand**: Ay, he left his old religion for an estate, and has not had time to get a new one.

Barker-Caven's point that Sheridan's irony is directed against Isaac as an individual whose financial opportunism exceeds his love of country or religion is persuasive. The depiction of Isaac is disturbing, however, precisely because anti-Semitic propaganda frequently asserts that Jewish people are financially motivated and have no loyalty to their native country. Conversely, Isaac is not portrayed as a malevolent villain. Louisa claims that Isaac is 'generally the dupe of his own art' and he duly schemes his way into marrying the penniless Margaret. The part of Isaac in the first production went to the popular comic actor John Quick, who became one of the most highly paid actors of his generation. According to Mark S. Auburn's essay

'Theatre in the Age of Garrick and Sheridan', found in *Sheridan Studies* (1995), 'He brought a turkey-cock air to low comic parts – country boobies, servants, old men, stage Jews and other exotics – and George III is said to have come to Covent Garden only to see Quick.' Sheridan used Quick for Bob Acres in *The Rivals* and Dr Rosy in *St Patrick's Day* and was certain of the actor's ability to win over an audience. Along with his fellow schemer, Jerome, Isaac is the most complex character in *The Duenna* and gets the best songs. His lyric in praise of ugly women recalls Jack's preference for women with two eyes ('the prejudice has always run in favour of *two*') in *The Rivals*:

> Give Isaac the nymph who no beauty can boast,
> But health and good humour to make her his toast.
> If straight, I don't mind whether slender or fat;
> And six feet or four – we'll never quarrel for that.
> For in eyes, though so various in lustre and hue,
> I swear I've no choice – only let her have two.

If Isaac has the greatest vitality in *The Duenna*, Jerome achieves the most variety of tone. Jerome resembles Sir Anthony Absolute in *The Rivals*. Both are widowers with a low opinion of women. Jerome's insistence that he married for money may be taken at face value but some actors have portrayed him as a man embittered by his refusal to acknowledge his grief over his dead wife:

> I married her for her fortune, and she took me in obedience to her father, and a very happy couple we were. We never expected any love from one another, and so we were never disappointed.

His song about his daughter's ingratitude in refusing the rich husband he has selected anticipates the views of the grotesque but perversely admirable patrician figures in Gilbert and Sullivan's Savoy Operas:

> When scarce in their teens they have wit to perplex us;
> With letters and lovers forever they vex us,
> While each still rejects the fair suitor you've brought her.
> O, what a plague is an obstinate daughter.
> > Wrangling and jangling,
> > Flouting and pouting,
> O, what a plague is an obstinate daughter.

Jerome is exceptional in his disregard for questions of social status. This is especially notable in a Spanish Comedy, a genre in which family honour is a major theme. He does not care whether Louisa's husband comes from a 'good' family, his only concern is for money. He praises England as a financially minded country: 'in England they were formerly as nice as to birth and family as we are; but they have long discovered what a wonderful purifier gold is, and now no one there regards pedigree in anything but a horse.'

The four lovers in *The Duenna* are lightly drawn. Ferdinand's morbid jealousy is a stereotypical trait in Spanish Comedies (Don Felix in *The Wonder* is another example) but it also recalls Faulkland's anxieties in *The Rivals*. An exchange between Jerome and Ferdinand suggests that Antonio anticipates Charles in *The School for Scandal*, both are young men whose poverty is attributed by their enemies to libertine habits and by their friends to a good heart:

> **Ferdinand**: Antonio, sir, has many amiable qualities.
> **Jerome**: But he is poor. Can you clear him of that, I say? Is he not a gay, dissipated rake, who has squandered his patrimony?
> **Ferdinand**: Sir, he inherited but little; and that his generosity, more than his profuseness has stripped him of.

Louisa and Clara are almost interchangeable. This makes the plot's confusion of identity between the two escaping heroines more plausible and allows for a comic encounter in which each woman believes that the other is more virtuous than she really is:

> **Louisa**: [aside] Clara is of a cold temper, and would think this step of mine highly forward.
> **Clara**: [aside] Louisa's respect for her father is so great, she would not credit the unkindness of mine.
> **Louisa**: You will be more surprised when I tell you that I have run away from my father.
> **Clara**: Surprised indeed! And I should certainly chide you most horribly, only that I have just run away from mine.

Although the play is set in Catholic Spain, Louisa and Clara are as hard-headedly secular as Jerome. Louisa declares that 'Why, to be sure, the character of a nun is a very becoming one, at a masquerade; but no pretty woman in her senses ever thought of taking the veil for above a night.' In the gloomiest song in the opera, Clara bids farewell to the convent where she took refuge: 'Adieu, thou dreary pile, where never dies/The sullen echo of repentant sighs.' This bleak view of the religious life belongs to a comic tradition which sees marriage rather than chastity as the fit end for a heroine's adventures. (In Shakespeare's *A Midsummer Night's Dream*, Theseus gives a dismal picture of Hermia's future if she becomes a nun instead of marrying the man her father has chosen: 'To live a barren sister all your life/Chanting faint hymns to the cold fruitless moon.') Louisa's claim that 'in religion, as in friendship, they who profess most are ever the least sincere' is a truism of Restoration Comedy, in which displays of piety are usually hypocritical but much of the third act of *The Duenna* is given over to specifically anti-Catholic satire. Unlike his 'repentant' nuns, Sheridan's monks drink heavily, make sexually suggestive toasts ('I'll give you the blue-eyed nun of St Catherine's') and appropriate legacies left to them for devotional purposes to pay their wine merchant. This satiric episode has no relevance to the plot of the play and was usually cut when *The Duenna* was performed in Catholic countries. It was inspired by John Dryden's depiction of the obese, corrupt and murderous Father Dominick (derived in turn from Shakespeare's Falstaff) in *The Spanish Friar* (1681), one of the very few of Dryden's plays still performed at the end of the eighteenth century. Sheridan's Friar Paul urbanely reinterprets his fat and wine-flushed appearance as evidence of his piety:

> **Paul**: Bloated I am, indeed, for fasting is a windy recreation, and it hath swollen me like a bladder.
> **Antonio**: But thou hast a good fresh colour in thy face, father. Rosy, i'faith!
> **Paul**: Yes, I have blushed for mankind, till the hue of my shame is as fixed as their vices.

Sheridan's love of such self-indulgent characters as Friar Paul attracted him to John Vanbrugh's *The Relapse*, which includes the flamboyant and egocentric Lord Foppington. Garrick had kept Vanbrugh's other major comedy, *The Provoked Wife* (1697), in the Drury Lane repertoire through his portrayal of Sir John Brute. Unfortunately, *The Relapse* contains two plots; the first in which Lord Foppington is outwitted by his younger brother, Young Fashion, has a broad comic appeal but the second plot, in which Berinthia and

Worthy conspire to seduce a husband and wife, Loveless and Amanda, would have been regarded by Georgian audiences as indecent. Consequently Sheridan rewrote the play as *A Trip to Scarborough*. His alterations fall into two categories. Firstly, there are the structural changes. *The Relapse* is a loosely knit work in which the two plots are almost unrelated. Sheridan reversed the priority given to these plots (the subplot about Lord Foppington becomes the dominant story) and created a greater interdependence between the two story lines by making Loveless into Young Fashion's friend. Secondly, Sheridan toned down the sexual content. Loveless is no longer a reformed libertine, willingly seduced by Berinthia (causing the relapse of Vanbrugh's title). Instead he is a previously faithful husband, who is surprised by the strength of his attraction to Berinthia. Worthy is renamed Townly and no longer conspires with Berinthia to divide the married couple. Townly and Berinthia have quarrelled and they independently make advances to Amanda and Loveless as a way of scoring off each other. While Amanda rejects Worthy at the end of *The Relapse* but is left with the bitter knowledge of her husband's infidelity, in *A Trip to Scarborough* no one commits adultery. Sheridan's ending is both structurally and morally neater: Loveless and Amanda resume their marriage with a deeper mutual appreciation, while Townly and Berinthia are reunited. Sheridan also tones down the cynicism of the marriage between Young Fashion and Hoyden. In *The Relapse* Young Fashion only wants Hoyden's money while she craves a life of freedom in London instead of remaining the near prisoner of her grotesque father, Sir Tunbelly Clumsy. Sheridan's version suggests that Young Fashion and Hoyden will raise a family together.

A Trip to Scarborough had a precarious first night on the 24 February 1777. Paula Byrne in *Perdita: The Life of Mary Robinson* (2004) recounts the events from the perspective of Mary Robinson, who played Amanda:

> The play was announced as a new piece under the title *A Trip to Scarborough*. The audience were furious when they realized that they had been duped and began hissing (ladies usually hissed through their fans). The leading actress, Mary Ann Yates, swept off stage, leaving Mary to 'encounter the critical tempest' alone. The terrified Mary was rooted to the spot, but Sheridan – from the side wing – bade her to stay on the stage.

The evening was saved when the Duke of Cumberland called to Mary from a side box: 'It is not you, but the play, they hiss.' She instinctively curtsied to the Duke and the audience applauded in amusement and let the play continue. The public's collective anger over being 'duped' by Sheridan, who had passed off a rewrite of an old play as his own work, suggests the ambivalent and sometimes threatening relationship between a theatre manager and his audience. It also gave Sheridan the incentive to finish *The School for Scandal* in just over two months, so that he could present a play that was unambiguously his own in early May.

After its hesitant start *A Trip to Scarborough* continued to be staged in Britain until the 1950s. It fell out of fashion with the rise of the permissive society. John Loftis asserts that 'We prefer Vanbrugh's uninhibited depiction of sexual subjects to Sheridan's muted and at times evasive depiction of them.' This statement invites a series of questions. Who are the 'we' Loftis mentions? Is an uninhibited treatment of sex necessarily better than a 'muted' one? Are 'we' underestimating the value of Sheridan's subtlety? Loftis demonstrates the slipperiness of 'we' when he adds that 'in at least one instance, we may consider Sheridan's bowdlerization as a gain. Even in this emancipated age, many do not relish the depiction of male homosexuality.' In *The Relapse* the marriage broker Coupler is explicit in his sexual advances to Young Fashion. Sheridan removed the homosexual content by turning Coupler into a woman. It is doubtful that replacing a flamboyant cameo role with a bland one is ever a gain. In Trevor Nunn's 2001 production of *The Relapse*, for instance, Edward Petherbridge's portrayal of Coupler became, according to Rhoda Koenig in the *Independent* (25 July 2001), 'the most screaming performance' in the play and 'had the house roaring'.

Sheridan redrafted Vanbrugh's sprawling play into a unified and tightly organised comedy but he deprived *The Relapse* of its anarchic energy. Vanbrugh's uncomfortable questions about marital fidelity are suppressed. Equally, in the subplot, when Young Fashion travels to Tunbelly Hall from London to marry Hoyden, Vanbrugh comically suggests a journey to the most uncivilised and benighted corner of the country. In *A Trip to Scarborough* Clod Hill is 'not a five minute drive' from town. England has shrunk and Vanbrugh's comic monsters, Lord Foppington, Sir Tunbelly Clumsy and Coupler dwindle into amiable eccentrics.

A Trip to Scarborough is most successful when Sheridan turns the prudery of his audience to his own advantage. It becomes a study in what is unsaid both in sexual relationships and on the Georgian stage. In his Prologue to the play David Garrick initially argues that notions of sexual decency are comparative, like fashions in dress they change with the times, but he finally supports the revision of plays in favour of an aesthetic of sexual restraint: 'Those writers well and wisely used their pens,/Who turn our wantons into magdalens'. (The Biblical reference is to Mary Magdalen, the prostitute who repented her sins on meeting Christ.) By implication, the portrayal of sexually adventurous women is acceptable on the stage providing they repent by the final act. Vanbrugh's Berinthia seduces a married man, enjoys the sex and shows no remorse, so she is unacceptable. Sheridan's Berinthia flirts with Loveless but becomes ashamed of herself, so she is acceptable. Sheridan follows Vanbrugh to a surprising extent in depicting Berinthia's sexual history. In both plays, she detested her husband (they 'Never agreed but once, which was about lying alone'). She has awoken to new sexual possibilities and provocatively tells Amanda that 'it's a delicious thing to be a young widow.' Neither woman is entirely repulsed by the idea of infidelity:

> **Amanda**: The practical part of all unlawful love is –
> **Berinthia**: O 'tis abominable; but for the speculative, that we must all confess is entertaining enough.

A similar tension between the 'practical' and the 'speculative' appeal of adultery informs Lady Teazle's relationship with Joseph Surface.

On their first appearance in *A Trip to Scarborough* Loveless and Amanda discuss going to the theatre. Amanda dislikes 'those empty pleasures which 'tis so much the fashion to be fond of.' She adds that 'Plays, I must confess, have some small charms, and would have more, would they restrain that loose encouragement to vice, which shocks, if not the virtue of some women, at least the modesty of all.' Amanda places herself in a long moral tradition which sees the portrayal of criminal or immoral actions on the stage as an 'encouragement to vice'. She favours the sentimental style of drama in which virtuous characters are rewarded, evil ones are punished and vice is not presented graphically. She adopts the conventional eighteenth-century position that women should be shielded from displays of immorality. Revealingly, she expresses some duplicity: even if women are not really shocked by immoral scenes, they should demonstrate their 'modesty' by appearing to be upset. Loveless argues that some great plays of the past might still be enjoyed if they received 'a little wholesome pruning' (the phrase is Sheridan's) to cut any indecencies. Sheridan suggests that his play is an example of such pruning but he also questions the standards he apparently upholds. Amanda is presented as a moral example (a similar role to Julia in *The Rivals* or Maria in *The School for Scandal*) but she believes that women should playact virtuous outrage even when they do not feel it. After expressing her disapproval of vice on the stage, she admits to Berinthia that Townly has been 'tampering' with her virtue by declaring his love. If Joseph Surface in *The School for Scandal* is a conscious hypocrite, Amanda is a self-deluded one. The quartet of lovers in *A Trip to Scarborough* act on motives that they will not entirely admit to themselves. Townly reveals this when he declares that, having been neglected by Berinthia, he is 'diverting my chagrin by offering up chaste incense to the beauties of Amanda, our friend Loveless's wife.' It is difficult to be 'chaste' while making adulterous advances. Sheridan's one major addition to Vanbrugh's story is a scene in a moonlit garden at the beginning of the fifth act in which the lovers stumble on each other, conceal themselves in the shadows and overhear each other's conversations. This is as near as they come to talking honestly.

If the four lovers in *A Trip to Scarborough* contributed to the adultery theme in *The School for Scandal*, the second plot in which two brothers seek to marry the same heiress foreshadows the love triangle between Joseph, Maria and Charles. Sheridan follows Vanbrugh in suggesting that Lord Foppington deserves to be outwitted. Young Fashion has 'scruples' about the deception until his elder brother's appallingly selfish behaviour eases his conscience. *The School for Scandal* reverses the position: the 'good' brother Charles is the victim of Joseph's duplicity. Young Fashion and Charles are generic *jeune premier* roles, high-spirited young men who have been impoverished by recklessness and generosity but who will supposedly soon settle down. In theatrical terms Foppington and Joseph are more compelling characters than their younger brothers. Even in Sheridan's toned-down version, Foppington conveys the extravagance and brutality of a man of fashion. In one of Sheridan's additions to the text, Foppington admits to his passion for gambling: 'Not that I ever play deep; indeed I have been for some time tied up from losing above five thousand pawnds at a sitting.' In 1777, five thousand pounds would have been a staggering amount. Hoyden's fortune amounts to three thousand a year and in Jane Austen's *Sense and Sensibility* (1811), Elinor believes that a family can live very comfortably on a thousand pounds a year. Sheridan is not, however, exaggerating the eighteenth-century passion for gambling. The immensely rich leader of the Whig party, Charles James Fox, repeatedly bankrupted himself because of his love of cards. Like Fox, Foppington's extravagant clothing qualifies him as a 'Macaroni', a descendent of the Restoration Fop and a predecessor to the Regency Beau. (Sir Benjamin Backbite mentions macaronies in his awful impromptu poem about Lady Betty Curricle's ponies in *The School for Scandal*.) Foppington's explanation of why he propositions Amanda has a convincing touch of arrogance: 'Because she was a woman of an insolent virtue, and I thought myself piqued in honour to debauch her.' Joseph shows a similar sadistic streak in anticipating how Lady Teazle will be in his power after sleeping with him. Despite Hoyden's naïve wish to marry a lord, her nurse predicts the life the young girl would experience with Lord Foppington: 'though these lords have a power of wealth indeed, yet, as I have heard say, they give it all to their sluts and their trulls'. The Nurse's evocation of an aristocratic marriage, in which the neglected wife sits at home while her husband spends her money on his mistresses, is a rare example of plain-speaking in a play where the characters usually restrict themselves to genteel hints.

The casting of Frances Abington as both Hoyden and the first Lady Teazle suggests Sheridan's awareness of the continuity between the two characters. According to Katharine Worth's *Sheridan and Goldsmith* (1992) Abington was 'renowned for her special brand of seductive charm'. This sensual quality would have been right for both Hoyden and Lady Teazle. When the Nurse tells Young Fashion how appealing Hoyden was as a baby, the heiress suggestively interrupts: 'If you have a mind to make him have a good opinion of a woman, don't tell him what one did then; tell him what one can do now.' Moments before, Hoyden has declared that 'I never disobey my father in anything but eating green gooseberries.' She is poised between a girlhood in which eating gooseberries is of great importance and an awareness of her developing sexuality ('what one can do now'). Hoyden wants to go to London to become a woman of fashion, the play ends as she is about to achieve her goal. Conversely Lady Teazle is a woman of fashion who hates to be reminded of her country upbringing. Joseph attributes her reluctance to commit adultery to the 'ill effects' of her 'country education'. Although Lady Teazle and Hoyden are not the same person, Sheridan suggests a line of development by casting Abington in both roles. *The School for Scandal* becomes a play about what an independently minded woman from the country, with money and a newly acquired social status, 'can do now' in London.

4

The School for Scandal

The School for Scandal (1777) is the first of Sheridan's plays to be set in London. The Comedy of Manners in England had always seen its natural home as the capital. The antagonism between the City in the East (the financial district, largely contained in the Roman city walls) and the West End of the court, aristocratic society and parliament, had been a comic standby since Ben Jonson wrote his City comedies at the beginning of the seventeenth century. If the characters in such plays did not live in the City or the West End, then they probably had lodgings by the Strand, the connecting route running alongside the Thames. Londoners were (as they still are) acutely aware of the importance of having a fashionable address, even to living on the right side of a particular street. The city provides its own language of semi-private references derived from a fusion of geography, social status and snobbery.

George Farquhar's *The Recruiting Officer* (1706) and *The Beaux' Stratagem* (1707) took the Comedy of Manners out of London and into the smaller communities of Shrewsbury and Lichfield with their rigid social structures. Oliver Goldsmith's *She Stoops to Conquer* (1773) had built on Farquhar's work to suggest the vitality of the country. If London had 'wit', the country had the less incisive but more forgiving trait of 'humour'. Sheridan in *The Rivals* and *A Trip to Scarborough* followed Farquhar in setting his work in small but fashionable communities. With *The School for Scandal* Sheridan returned the Comedy of Manners to its home. Lady Teazle's horror at the memory of her rural past reflects the hatred of the country of numerous Restoration Comedy heroines, such as Harriet in George Etherege's *The Man of Mode* (1676).

Most of the characters in *The School for Scandal* could be assumed to live close to the Drury Lane Theatre where the play was first performed on 8 May 1777. It became the most frequently performed play of the last twenty-five years of the eighteenth century and helped to bring in the crowds whenever Drury Lane was short of funds.

Even more than Sheridan's previous works, *The School for Scandal* embodies a fusion of the old and the very new. It freely borrows characters and situations from seventeenth-century plays. The idea of a 'school' or academy governed by women had long been the subject of satire. Jonson's *Epicoene* (1609) included a Ladies Collegiate, Molière mocked female-dominated literary coteries in *Les Femmes savantes* (1672) and William Wycherley's *The Country Wife* (1675) contained a 'virtuous gang' of sex-hungry married women. According to this misogynistic tradition, such female gatherings were at best mistaken in their principles and made themselves ridiculous by misunderstanding the knowledge they sought to acquire. At worst, the women merely covered for each other's extra-marital affairs. In Sheridan's play, the school's principal, Lady Sneerwell, is based on Farquhar's similarly named Lady Lurewell in *The Constant Couple* (1699). Lady Sneerwell's malice derives from when she was the innocent victim of a scandal; Lady Lurewell is equally malicious towards all men because she was seduced as a young woman and then abandoned.

The unhappy marriage of an ageing man to a much younger wife is a frequent trope in Restoration plays. Sir Peter and Lady Teazle are largely based on Sir John and Lady Brute in John Vanbrugh's *The Provoked Wife* (1697). Sir Peter's opening speech resembles Sir John's complaints about matrimony at the beginning of Vanbrugh's play. Here is Sir John:

> What cloying meat is love, when matrimony's the sauce to it! Two years' marriage has debauched my five senses. Everything I see, everything I hear, everything I feel, everything I smell, and everything I taste, methinks has wife in't. No boy was ever so weary of his tutor, no girl of her bib, no nun of doing penance, or old maid of being chaste, as I am of being married. Sure, there's a secret curse entailed upon the very name of wife. My lady is a young lady, a fine lady, a witty lady, a virtuous lady, and yet, I hate her. There is but one thing on earth I loath beyond her, that's fighting. Would my courage come up to a fourth part of my ill-nature, I'd stand buff to her relations, and thrust her out of doors.

Here is Sir Peter on his matrimonial problems:

When an old bachelor marries a young wife, what is he to expect? 'Tis now six months since Lady Teazle made me the happiest of men – and I have been the miserablest dog since we committed matrimony. We tiffed a little going to church, and came to a quarrel before the bells were done ringing. I was more than once nearly choked with gall during the honeymoon, and had lost all comfort in life before my friends had done wishing me joy. Yet I chose with caution – a girl bred wholly in the country, who never knew luxury beyond one silk gown, nor dissipation above the annual gala of a race ball. Yet now she plays her part in all the extravagant fopperies of the fashion and the town, with as ready a grace as if she had never seen a bush nor a grass-plot out of Grosvenor Square. I am sneered at by all my acquaintance and paragraphed in the newspapers. She dissipates my fortune and contradicts all my humours. Yet the worst of it is, I doubt I love her, or I should never bear all this. However, I'll never be weak enough to own it.

Sir John Brute had been one of David Garrick's favourite roles. He first played the part in 1744 and he kept it in the Drury Lane repertoire for the rest of his career. There is a painting by Zoffany of Garrick, red-faced and cross-dressed, as Sir John from 1765. Sheridan would have expected his Drury Lane audience to recognise both the parallel and the crucial differences between the two ageing husbands. Sir John, as his surname suggests, is a more brutal character. Although a self-confessed coward, he imagines throwing his blameless wife out of the house and defying her relatives. He takes refuge from his frustration in heavy drinking. Sir Peter, in contrast, may be infuriated by his wife's behaviour but he does not contemplate physical violence or wish to be rid of her. Sheridan artfully suggests Sir Peter's salvation in this opening speech: once he becomes 'weak enough' to reveal his love for his wife, a reconciliation will be possible. In Restoration Comedies these older husbands were usually cuckolded – Sir John and Sir Peter narrowly avoid the same fate. Lady Brute's adultery is prevented by a comic mischance while Lady Teazle discovers Joseph's duplicity even as he attempts to seduce her.

Sir Peter and Lady Teazle are also comparable to Pinchwife and Margery in William Wycherley's *The Country Wife*. Pinchwife, like Sir Peter, has married a much younger woman from the country whom he wrongly thinks he can control. In Wycherley's play, Margery and the libertine Horner cuckold Pinchwife. Sheridan's depiction of

Joseph's failure to bed Lady Teazle is an indicator of how the audience's morality had changed. As Ann Blake, the editor of the New Mermaid edition (2004) of the play states: 'a comedy in which she was seduced would not have been acceptable to Sheridan's audience.' The play however gives some contradictory evidence about Lady Teazle's fidelity. Ostensibly, Joseph has often entreated her to see his library (a pretext for getting her alone) and she has refused until Sir Peter's accusations goad her into changing her mind. But Joseph's servant declares that 'she always leaves her chair at the milliner's in the next street', implying that she has visited Joseph repeatedly while pretending to have a different destination.

The sexual reticence in *The School for Scandal* works in Sheridan's favour. The scandalmongers make their rumours more potent by furnishing hints rather than outright statements, especially in a society where, among men and women of the world, some things are assumed to be so obvious that they need not be spelled out. Sir Peter for instance is not overly surprised when he believes that Joseph has a 'French Milliner' hidden in his room and does not question Joseph's high moral reputation because of the discovery. It is entirely acceptable for a young gentleman to have discreet affairs with working women.

George Bernard Shaw, among others, recognised that the contrast between the profligate but kind Charles and the cold-blooded Joseph resembles that of Tom and his hypocritical brother Blifil in Henry Fielding's novel *Tom Jones* (1749). Fielding, though, was a dramatist before he became a novelist; he derived his characters from previous theatrical stereotypes. William Congreve's plays also influenced the creation of the two brothers. Charles' poverty, his generosity and his romantic (but not necessarily sexual) devotion to one woman recall Valentine in *Love for Love* (1695), while Joseph resembles the hypocrite Maskwell in *The Double Dealer* (1693). Both Maskwell and Joseph bring their downfall on themselves by simultaneously attempting to seduce a married woman and trying to steal a young heiress' affections away from the man she loves. The opposition between brothers, though, has an archetypal appeal. Critics including Bernard Shaw have often pointed out the doubtful logic of Sir Oliver's tests. Charles is hardly proved 'good' because he will not sell a painting of his uncle and Joseph is not necessarily 'bad' because he refuses to give money to an impoverished kinsman. Sheridan is however evoking the symbolic justice of the tests in fairy tales where the elder brothers fail through selfishness or ingratitude while the youngest brother succeeds with an impulsive act of kindness.

Despite the extent of Sheridan's borrowing from previous plays, his contemporaries saw *The School for Scandal* as a very modern work. Appropriately, the play's early popularity was partially due to a growing scandal. It was assumed that the characters were based on Sheridan's friends in the Devonshire House Circle. Amanda Foreman in her biography *Georgiana, Duchess of Devonshire* (1998) claims that 'Sheridan pandered to the audience's expectations by portraying Georgiana's friends as a set of louche aristocrats whose moral sensibilities had been blunted by a life of wealth without responsibility. Georgiana is Lady Teazle: young, easily influenced, possessed of a good heart but needing a firm husband to manage her properly.' Sheridan's political allies, including Georgiana, went to Drury Lane to see themselves portrayed on stage. Their attendance reflects the ambivalent attitude of Sheridan's world to gossip and scandal. As Foreman claims 'eighteenth-century society tolerated anything so long as there was no scandal. Publicly immoral behaviour earned public censure; private transgression remained whispered gossip.' Georgiana in reaction to her husband's infidelities was testing the limits of discretion; her adventures were discussed in the gossip sheets with a mixture of moral disapproval and salacious pleasure. Since Sheridan was the lover of Frances Crewe (to whom he dedicated *The School for Scandal*), a leading member of the Devonshire House Circle, and was later to have an affair with Georgiana's younger sister, Lady Duncannon, he was complicit in the behaviour that fuelled the developing scandal.

The modernity of *The School for Scandal* involves its treatment of the power of the media as an arbiter of morality and even of reality. Lady Sneerwell refers to the recently established newspapers which printed scandal in the first line of the play. The scandalous *Town and Country Magazine*, mentioned in this opening conversation, was founded in 1769 only eight years before Sheridan's play was staged. Londoners were entering into a new and worryingly intimate relationship with the media. Sir Peter in his monologue complains that his marriage is 'paragraphed in the newspapers'. He is the subject of printed gossip. The conspiracy to divide Charles and Maria fails but the harmfulness of the anonymous letters written by Snake and Lady Sneerwell, claiming that Lady Teazle is having an affair with Charles, should not be underestimated. The imaginary duel involving

Sir Peter in the last act provides some high comedy but it is based on a genuine danger. A gentleman who discovered that his wife was unfaithful would be expected to challenge the lover to a duel. The publication of insinuations about adultery in the newspapers made the situation more serious by involving the entire community. It put considerable pressure on the wronged husband to defend his honour. (After his elopement, Sheridan challenged Captain Mathews to a duel after Mathews publically insulted him in the *Bath Chronicle*.) If Lady Sneerwell's forgeries had been successful they might have resulted in the death of Charles or Sir Peter.

Sheridan's comedy has a serious edge in its delineation of the power of both rumour and the press. The opening scene of the play allows the gossipmongers to demonstrate their influence. Crabtree's story of Miss Piper and the Nova Scotia sheep is a gleeful account of how a scandal ruins the innocent Miss Piper's reputation and her marriage prospects (she lost 'her lover and her character'). One aspect of scandal is its attitude of moral superiority. Over a century later, Oscar Wilde distinguished between scandal and gossip in his first comedy, *Lady Windermere's Fan* (1892):

> **Cecil Graham**: Oh! gossip is charming! History is merely gossip. But scandal is gossip made tedious by morality. Now, I never moralize. A man who moralizes is usually a hypocrite, and a woman who moralizes is invariably plain.

Wilde suggests that beneath its surface morality, scandal is motivated by a mixture of hypocrisy and sexual envy. These motivations drive the plot of *The School for Scandal*. Joseph, the hypocrite, wants Maria's fortune and Lady Sneerwell wants to displace Maria in Charles' affections. Sheridan does not, however, suggest that an audience can comfortably pass its own moral judgement on the scandalmongers. Their grotesque energy and creativity is too entertaining. The reviews of John Gielgud's 'all-star' production of the play which opened on 5 April 1962 at the Theatre Royal, Haymarket, focused on Margaret Rutherford's Mrs Candour who, according to the unsigned review in *The Times* could be seen 'sucking up scandal like a fish sucking its way around a glass aquarium.' Caryl Brahms' review of Rutherford in the same production reveals how a supporting character can offer a thematic key to the play: 'her glee in sniffing the sweet incense of some wrecked reputation is equalled only by our own as we watch suspicions becoming certainties.' As an audience we become complicit in Mrs Candour's quest for titillating details. Matthew Bevis argues in *Comedy: A Very Short Introduction* (2013) that our complicity is central to Sheridan's intention:

> We may deride Mrs Candour's hypocrisy as she listens to the gossip – 'Ha, ha, ha! Well, you make me laugh; but I vow I hate you for't' – but she is our twin. The sheer sparkle of the malice is what we have come to listen to, and in this environment to be a witness is to be an accomplice.

One of the running jokes of *The School for Scandal* is that scandal is an Art form and its major practitioners deserve to be venerated. At the beginning of the play, Snake appropriates terms from eighteenth-century Art criticism in preferring Lady Sneerwell's style of scandal to Mrs Clackit's: 'her colouring is too dark and her outline often extravagant. She wants that delicacy of Hint – and mellowness of sneer which distinguish your Ladyship's Scandal.' Snake's pictorial terms refer to another recently established 'school'. The Royal Academy of Arts was founded in December 1768 and the once-yearly lectures, the *Discourses*, by its first president, Sir Joshua Reynolds, had an important cultural influence. (Sheridan slips a compliment to Reynolds, the 'Modern Raphael', into the picture scene later in the play.) Crabtree's account of the fictitious duel between Charles and Sir Peter is a masterpiece of pictorial detail and can earn a round of applause in performance. The mention of the 'bronze Shakespeare' is an ironic tribute to the artistry of gossip:

> **Crabtree**: A pair of pistols lay on the bureau (for Mr Surface, it seems had come there the night before late from Salthill, where he had been to see the Montem with a friend, who has a son at Eton) so, unluckily the pistols were left charged.
> **Sir Benjamin**: I heard nothing of this.
> **Crabtree**: Sir Peter forced Charles to take one, and they fired, it seems, pretty nearly together. Charles's shot took place, as I told you, and Sir Peter's missed; but, what is very extraordinary, the ball struck against a little bronze Shakespeare that stood over the fireplace, grazed out of the window at a right angle, and wounded the postman, who was just coming to the door with a double letter from Northamptonshire.

Crabtree may believe his fantastic story. The Age of Reason was also an age of fantasists. The mystic Count Cagliostro was in London when *The School for Scandal* was first staged and Baron Münchausen (the 'lying Baron') was telling the tall stories which would inspire Rudolph Erich Raspe's *Baron Munchausen's Narrative of his Marvellous Travels* (1785). Ian Kelly in his biography *Beau Brummell* (2005) takes a positive view of the insubstantiality of people's reputations in Sheridan's play, focusing on the freedom that gossip and fantasy gave an urban population to fashion new identities:

> Hypocritical, sardonic and blithe by turns, the Surface brothers, Charles and Joseph, were true modern Londoners. Nothing was quite what it seemed anymore – reputation and reality were changing fast in the new West End where the old, intimate moral certainties were gone for ever. But the explosive impact of *The School for Scandal* was as joyous as it was shocking. It was a liberating thought for young Londoners that they could create themselves, and rejoice in their escape from 'moral rigorism'.

It is intriguing that Kelly does not distinguish between the 'Surface brothers'. They are both 'Hypocritical, sardonic and blithe by turns'. At the centre of the play is the tide of public opinion flowing around these enigmatic brothers. In the final act virtue (Charles) is rewarded and vice (Joseph) is exposed but the play is not quite so clear-cut. Charles does not appear until the beginning of Act Three (approximately an hour into the performance of the play) although he is mentioned frequently as a 'libertine' in the first two acts. Appropriately, in a play about scandal, the hero is more talked about than seen. His character depends on the director of an individual production as much as the playwright. If his drinking party consists of only a few tipsy men singing a suggestive song (there are no speaking roles for women in the scene), then Charles' 'libertinism' might be a slander spread by Joseph and Lady Sneerwell. Conversely, if the director introduces prostitutes joining in the song and caressing the men, as happened in Elizabeth Freestone's Greenwich Theatre production of 2010, then Charles' bad reputation might be deserved and his devotion to Maria becomes dubious. Michael Billington has noted how amenable the play is to 'differently slanted interpretations':

In 1949 Laurence Olivier directed *The School for Scandal* for the Old Vic in glittering bandbox Cecil Beaton sets and costumes. In 1972 Jonathan Miller directed it for the National Theatre Company with the Teazles living in a draughty, rundown mansion full of grimy ancestral portraits and with Charles Surface steeped in Hogarthian squalor – discarded girls dead drunk on the floor and the house half-demolished to pay for the debauchery.

Often directors of *The School for Scandal* have taken a deliberately stylised approach to highlight certain themes. Peter Wood's production at the National Theatre in 1990 included furniture covered with oversized newsprint to suggest how the media influences our perception of reality. Freestone's 2010 production colour-coded the characters' costumes. The scandalmongers wore green, for instance, suggestive of the envy that motivates them and struck rock-star poses on first greeting each other to convey their exaggerated sense of self-importance. Deborah Warner's controversial 2011 production of the play at the Barbican Centre, London took Freestone's contemporary touches further. It contributed to the recurring debate about whether Sheridan's plays can be successfully modernised or whether they need their eighteenth-century trappings. Warner's gossipmongers carry Gucci handbags, Charles dances manically to club music and Joseph in the screen scene is engaged in penetrative sex with Lady Teazle just as Sir Peter arrives. Brechtian captions punctuated the scenes. According to the Barbican's promotional material the production drew parallels between Sheridan's salon culture, the catwalk and 'today's cocaine-driven clubland'. Some critics were extremely hostile. Charles Spencer, for instance, in the *Telegraph* (23 May 2011) called it 'one of the most arrogant and inept productions of a classic it has ever been my misfortune to witness.' He added that 'Watching this *School for Scandal* is like witnessing a group of louts spray-painting an elegant old building with graffiti.' (Essentially Spencer accuses Warner of cultural vandalism.) Warner's reply to her critics, '*The School for Scandal* storm in an eighteenth-century teacup', in the *Guardian* of 1 June 2011 upheld a director's right to explore a canonical text for contemporary relevance: 'We revive old plays because we think they may have something to say to us now.' The ensuing controversy largely concerned the needs of a younger audience; Warner argued that she had made the play more accessible while Spencer and

Billington claimed that she was patronising younger people with her 'heavy-handed' approach. (A brief interview with Warner interspersed with clips of her production of *The School for Scandal* is posted on YouTube.) Whether a director favours Wood's subtle effects or Warner's provocative and confrontational ones, such visual interpolations reiterate that Sheridan's characters were dealing with a newly emerging world of media distortion. They emphasise the disorientating quality of late eighteenth-century society in which questions of personal reputation, privacy, morality and even identity become uncertain and changeable.

Bernard Shaw protests that the supposed contrast between Charles and Joseph only serves 'to demonstrate that a bad man is not so bad as a worse'. The two brothers have a disconcerting tendency to blur into each other. Their conversation about adultery, concerning Sir Peter and Lady Teazle, during the screen scene is particularly ambivalent:

> **Charles**: To be sure, I once thought the lady seemed to have taken a fancy to me; but, upon my soul, I never gave her the least encouragement. Besides, you know my attachment to Maria.
> **Surface**: But, sure, brother, even if Lady Teazle had betrayed the fondest partiality for you –
> **Charles**: Why, look'ee, Joseph, I hope I shall never deliberately do a dishonourable action; but if a pretty woman was purposely to throw herself in my way – and that pretty woman married to a man old enough to be her father –
> **Surface**: Well?
> **Charles**: Why, I believe I should be obliged to borrow a little of your morality.

Charles asserts his innocence of any affair with Lady Teazle and his enduring love for Maria but he implies a good deal more. His cryptic remark about what he would do if a 'pretty woman married to a man old enough to be her father' were to 'throw herself' at him is an important example of Sheridan's ability to say – and avoid saying – several things at once. Charles hopes that he might refuse the temptation in the same way as his 'moral' brother would but the audience has just witnessed Joseph's attempt to seduce Lady Teazle. If Charles sees through his brother's hypocrisy then his remark is ironic, implying that neither man would refuse the opportunity for a discreet affair. They would act identically. James Roberts' painting from 1777 of the screen scene, based on the first production of *The School for Scandal*, suggests that Sheridan wanted the brothers to seem alike; the screen has just fallen, Lady Teazle stands near the centre of the composition with Sir Peter on her right, the brothers are on her left, in very similar positions, both looking away from her in the same direction. In *The Rivals*, Beverley and Jack Absolute are the same person; in *The School for Scandal* the brothers Joseph and Charles are two halves of one person; appropriately, they unite in Act Five in an attempt to push Sir Oliver out of their father's house.

Maria acts as the voice of morality in the play but she has never been a favourite with either audiences or actors. In a review of one performance of the part Shaw notes that 'Maria was hardly in Miss Brooke's line; but then Maria is not in anybody's line.' Her discussion about wit and malice in Act One with Lady Sneerwell and Joseph establishes Maria's uneasy relationship both with the gossipmongers and with the audience:

> **Maria**: Wit loses its respect with me when I see it in company with malice. – what do you think Mr Surface?
> **Surface**: Certainly, Madam, to smile at the jest which plants a Thorn in another's Breast is to become a principal in the Mischief.
> **Lady Sneerwell**: Pshaw! – there's no possibility of being witty – without a little ill-nature: the malice of a good thing is the Barb that makes it stick – what's your opinion Mr Surface?
> **Surface**: To be sure madam – that conversation where the Spirit of Raillery is suppress'd will ever appear tedious and insipid –

Joseph's hypocritical desire to agree with both Maria and Lady Sneerwell, even though they hold contrary views, is a revealing comic touch but it also indicates a contemporary dilemma about the nature of comedy. If human beings are essentially benign as eighteenth-century philosophers such as Lord Shaftesbury and Jean-Jacques Rousseau argue, then it seems odd that we laugh so readily at the misfortunes of others. Dramatists as diverse as Richard Steele and George Farquhar tried to replace the malice involved in wit (which ruthlessly strips people of their pretensions) with the genial laughter associated with humour. Maria shares this preference for humour. Lady Sneerwell argues that good comedy contains an element of cruelty. It may fulfil a moral function by exposing vice but that exposure is, in itself, cruel. Maria's views are to her credit morally but it is difficult to disagree with Lady Sneerwell. Ridicule and humiliation are powerful weapons for a comedian. A comedy in which the characters only said kind things to each other would, as Joseph suggests, be 'tedious and insipid'.

Joseph has many antecedents in seventeenth-century comedy. The unmasking of Joseph's hypocrisy resembles a similar screen scene in Molière's *Tartuffe*. Congreve's Maskwell in *The Double Dealer* is also exposed when two of his potential victims hide behind a screen and overhear him and his benefactor's wife discuss their sexual relationship. Farquhar's Vizard in *The Constant Couple* tries to disgrace the frank and open Sir Harry Wildair (a popular character with eighteenth-century audiences and a model for Charles Surface). Like Vizard and Maskwell, Joseph Surface's name comments on his duplicity. The Biblical Joseph refused the sexual advances of Potiphar's wife in *Genesis* chapter 39. Sheridan's Joseph offers an ironic contrast by attempting to seduce Lady Teazle but as soon as Joseph is categorised as a malevolent hypocrite, the definition seems inadequate.

Joseph's pursuit of Lady Teazle is surprisingly half-hearted. In a soliloquy which ends Act Two, Scene 1, he confesses that his involvement with her originated in a misunderstood gesture of politeness:

> I wanted at first only to ingratiate myself with Lady Teazle that she might not be my enemy with Maria; and I have, I don't know how, become her serious lover. Sincerely I begin to wish I had never made such a point of gaining so very good a character, for it has led me into so many cursed rogueries that I doubt I shall be exposed at last.

Joseph would not be the first or last person to say something out of politeness only to discover that an emotionally demanding person has treated it with misplaced seriousness. His prediction that his affair with Lady Teazle will lead to his exposure as a hypocrite is accurate but his puzzlement ('I don't know how') is curiously touching. His relationships with the other two women in whom he is supposed to have an erotic interest are even more remote. He wants Maria for her money, in pointed contrast to Lady Sneerwell, whose attraction to the penniless Charles is voraciously physical. Equally the first scene establishes that Joseph's romance with Lady Sneerwell is a fiction designed to give both characters the freedom to pursue other people.

Sheridan distinguishes Joseph from the conventional stage hypocrite by giving him a certain innocence. Despite his intelligence, he cannot understand why other people do not act with the same duplicity as he does. From a practical point of view, he is sensible in his wish to accumulate money, to discredit his potential enemies and to create a good impression in society. He may wonder why characters such as Lady Teazle, Charles and Maria make themselves so vulnerable by being so recklessly honest.

Although no one interpretation of a dramatic character should ever be exclusive, there is a tradition among actors and critics about how Joseph is most effectively performed. He is not an obvious, sneering and hand-wringing villain. The first actor to take on the role, John Palmer, was known by a couple of significant nicknames. He was 'Plausible Jack' (because of his much-praised performance in Wycherley's *The Plain Dealer* as Lord Plausible) and 'Gentleman Jack' because of his good manners and appearance of absolute frankness. Charles Lamb in his essay 'Some of the Old Actors' (1822) recalls Palmer's acting style: 'Jack had two voices – both plausible, hypocritical and insinuating'. Palmer used his 'two voices' to underscore Joseph's duplicity: 'The *sentiments* of Joseph Surface, were thus marked out in a sort of italics to the audience.' Similarly, the early twentieth-century actor-manager Sir Johnston Forbes-Robertson praises, in *A Player Under Three Reigns* (1925), the compassionate honesty that the Victorian actor Jack Clayton brought to the role:

> John Clayton was a very finished actor; his Joseph Surface was the finest I ever saw, full of subtlety and unction, and invested with all the fine airs one associates with the eighteenth century. He made it appear quite natural that Sir Peter should trust Joseph, so gracious and sincere was his behaviour to the older man.

It is important, as Forbes-Robertson suggests, that Sir Peter should not seem exceptionally gullible in trusting Joseph. Despite Lady Sneerwell's description of Joseph's duplicity in the opening scene, the audience should find itself almost seduced by his apparent honesty. Forbes-Robertson also became a celebrated Joseph and was praised by Shaw in *The Saturday Review* of 27 June 1896 for creating 'the most delicate hypocritical effect'. Forbes-Robertson was a very handsome actor and often embarrassed by the intensity of his women admirers. After playing Joseph, he played Hamlet for the first time and brought his considerable sex appeal to the melancholy Prince. Both Hamlet and Joseph pretend to read a book onstage to ward off suspicion from their actual intentions. Perhaps Joseph's noble 'sentiments' are a debased version of Hamlet's great soliloquies on the human condition.

In contrast to such comic moralists as Ben Jonson and William Wycherley, Sheridan does not greatly reward virtue or punish vice in the last act of his comedy. At the end of *The School for Scandal* the more sympathetic characters talk about their intentions rather than any fixed decisions. Charles ambivalently jokes about changing his behaviour after his marriage: 'Why, as to reforming, Sir Peter, I'll make no promises, and that I take to be a proof that I intend to set about it.' The Teazles 'intend' to live 'happily together'. Lady Sneerwell and Joseph are publically exposed but they are not, like Jonson's Volpone, stripped of their fortunes. Joseph even parodies the language of repentance: 'I confess I deviated from the direct road of wrong'. Snake tellingly echoes Joseph in his requests that his 'good deed' should never be revealed: 'if it were once known that I had been betrayed into an honest action, I should lose every friend I have in the world.' The scandalmongers are briefly routed but will continue to spread their gossip. Perhaps the most ambivalent figure on the stage at the end is Sir Oliver Surface. In archetypal terms, he is the wise old mentor who tests and financially rewards Charles for his good heart. Conversely, Sir Oliver has made his fortune in the East Indies; he is one of the despised 'nabobs' who were popularly suspected of exploiting the native population. (In the next decade Sheridan was to play a key part in prosecuting Warren Hastings, the Governor General of Bengal, a particularly eminent nabob.) It is possible that Sir Oliver's 'eastern liberality' derives from corrupt and inhumane business practices, in which case his testing of the moral virtue of Joseph and Charles is deeply ironic.

The Sheridaniana includes an anecdote in which Sheridan claims that, of all our passions, 'Vanity is the great commanding passion of all.' *The School for Scandal* can be read as a satire on vanity but without much confidence. The duplicitous Snake returns to 'the world', by which he means fashionable London society, while the virtuous Teazles resolve to leave for the countryside. Sheridan, however, as a young man with political ambitions remained firmly of 'the world'.

5

The Camp, The Critic and *Pizarro*

Sheridan's last three plays took a new direction in two important ways. Firstly, they convey an increasingly explicit political content. *The Camp* and *The Critic* make clear references to Britain's disastrous wars with the American colonies, while *Pizarro* explores the nature of colonialism. All three plays question the nature of patriotism, which at its best shows a selfless generosity of spirit but at its worst supports Samuel Johnson's claim that 'Patriotism is the last refuge of a scoundrel'. Secondly, these plays involved a greater use of theatrical spectacle than Sheridan's earlier work. This change resulted from his collaboration with Philippe Jacques de Loutherbourg, who is mentioned in both *The Camp* and *The Critic*. Garrick hired Loutherbourg as a scene designer for Drury Lane in 1771; the artist became renowned for the realism of his special effects.

Sheridan dashed off *The Camp: A Musical Entertainment* with his brother-in-law, Robert Tickell, as a response to contemporary events. It was first performed on 15 October 1778. France had allied itself with the United States compelling Britain to declare war in February 1778. The British, fearing a French invasion, established a series of military camps along the south coast; the largest was at Coxheath near Maidstone. Sheridan's political patroness, Georgiana, the Duchess of Devonshire, led a group of society women to Coxheath to boost morale. They wore dresses designed to suggest military uniforms and established a luxurious camp of their own. For her Whig allies, Georgiana's gesture demonstrated a laudable patriotism that overcame class barriers. For her enemies the exercise feminized war and made the army look ridiculous. Sheridan sent Loutherbourg to Coxheath to make sketches of the camp to guarantee the authenticity of its recreation on the Drury Lane stage. *The Camp* comments on the controversy created by this meeting between high fashion and military action. The play has two minimalistic plots; in the first a young soldier, William, is reunited with his sweetheart

Nancy, who is disguised as a boy, and in the second an Irish scenic painter called O'Daub is sent by Loutherbourg (anglicised into 'Leatherbag') to sketch the camp but is mistaken by the soldiers for a French spy. Both story lines are resolved by the benign intervention of Lady Plume, a fictionalized portrait of Georgiana.

Sheridan adopts an ambivalent stance towards patriotism by introducing several characters with differing reactions to the military camp. Lady Plume and Nell, a local woman, are idealistic patriots, lending the army their selfless support but most of the local people raise the price of their goods when selling them to the military. Ironically, the main supplier of food to the camp is a Frenchman. When he is asked if his nationality causes him a conflict of loyalty, Monsieur Bluard answers that his primary allegiance is to whoever wins: 'I never vil forsake your Camp if you vin the Battle – '. Sir Harry Bouquet lightly mocks the aristocratic ladies for their military pretensions: 'on the first sign of bad Weather you'll give orders to Strike your Toilets, and each secure a Retreat to Tunbridge.' The newspapers praised the play as a lightweight entertainment but the most enthusiastic responses were to Loutherbourg's stagecraft. His recreation of the Coxheath camp from several viewpoints was praised and his use of mechanised puppets to evoke a military drill seen in the distance was a technical triumph. When Sheridan staged *The Critic* he depended on Loutherbourg's assistance. The scenic artist's view of Tilbury Fort and his creation of the onstage naval battle which closes the play were widely celebrated.

The Critic was first staged on 30 October 1779 at Drury Lane after a performance of *Hamlet*. It was customary for a short sketch, the 'afterpiece', to follow the main play of the evening. Generally, these afterpieces were slight works, depending on spectacle or stage business to gain applause but Sheridan's play won an immediate reputation and continues to be admired. Lord Byron in his journal for 8 December 1813 claims that it is 'the best farce' ever written and declares it 'too good for an afterpiece'. In reviewing Laurence Olivier's production in 1945, Kenneth Tynan calls *The Critic* 'the wittiest play in English'. Tynan also discusses its lack of many of the conventional elements of dramatic writing:

> *The Critic* is one of the very smallest group of great plays in that it attains the most uproarious effects of fun by sheer verbal ingenuity. It has no 'situations', no plot, no shape, no development: it has only

words, and words chimed subtly together into a pattern of wit that Sheridan could never afterwards repeat.

In part, *The Critic* depends on its sheer self-conscious theatricality. It allows for a company, and particularly a lead actor, to dazzle by their virtuosity, especially if, following the tradition of its first night, it is performed immediately after a famous tragedy. Olivier staged *The Critic* in a double bill with Sophocles' *Oedipus Rex*. Melvyn Bragg in *Laurence Olivier* (1984) evokes the impact of this dual performance:

> He played Oedipus in Sophocles' *Oedipus Rex* and, having left the stage with bleeding eyes and a howl based on his imagined reproduction of the pain a fox felt with its leg caught in a steel trap, he reappeared fifteen minutes later as the ridiculously liveried, powdered and pomaded, flighty and sparklingly superficial Mr Puff, to be hoisted and shot and cannonballed around the stage like a rag doll.

As usual with Sheridan, his play is a mixture of canny topicality and Restoration theatrical sources. In 1779 Spain joined France in announcing its support for America and declared war on Britain. An invasion seemed imminent. It was feared that the British fleet was unprepared for battle even though Spanish and French ships were spotted in August in the English Channel. These concerns are mirrored in Dangle's opening complaint in Act One that the newspapers contain 'Nothing but about the fleet, and the nation!' and Mrs Dangle's gibe at her stage-struck husband that 'if the French were landed tomorrow, your first enquiry would be, whether they had brought a theatrical troupe with them.' The patriotic press made parallels with Queen Elizabeth's defiance of the Spanish Armada and the theatres staged Elizabethan pageants. By mid-autumn, the threat of invasion had dwindled and Londoners recalled the summer panic with irony. Covent Garden started its season in September with a jingoistic production of *Henry V* but by October it was staging Edward Neville's farce about invasion scares, *Plymouth in an Uproar*. At this point Sheridan wrote his own parody of a Spanish Armada tragedy for Drury Lane.

Knowing that his play was to follow *Hamlet*, Sheridan ensured a certain amount of crossover between the two productions as well as introducing other Shakespearean references. Ophelia and Tilburina probably wore the same white silk dress in their madness. More generally, *The Critic* evokes Shakespeare's meta-theatrical use of plays within a play. *Hamlet* contains both an extract from an unnamed Trojan play and *The Murder of Gonzago*. The performance of *Pyramus and Thisbe* in *A Midsummer Night's Dream* also ridicules overblown rhetorical tragedies in a way which anticipates Sheridan. Pyramus' 'O night which ever art when day is not' is similar to the tautological humour of the Governor's 'The Spanish fleet thou canst not see – because/– It is not yet in sight!'

Sheridan's chief inspiration for *The Critic* is *The Rehearsal* (1671) by George Villiers, the Duke of Buckingham. Villiers' play is set during a rehearsal at Drury Lane of a tragedy by an ambitious playwright called Bayes, who values theatrical novelty over sincerity and simplicity. Bayes reveals his crassness both in his claims of utter originality ('I tread upon no man's heels: but make my flight upon my own wings, I assure you') and his view that a play's story only serves as a pretext for impressive effects: 'what a Devil is the Plot good for, but to bring in fine things?' There is a strong element of class consciousness to *The Rehearsal*. Villiers the aristocrat and amateur playwright ridicules Bayes, the vulgar and upwardly mobile professional author.

The differences between Villiers and Sheridan are as revealing as their similarities. Unlike Sheridan, Villiers mocks bad theatrical writing from a neo-classical position inspired by Aristotle's *Poetics*. He believes that a tragedy should encompass a single unified plot, a limited number of characters and a conflict based on a rational dilemma. Consequently Bayes' play is a collection of all the Baroque mannerisms that Villiers thought ridiculous; it offers a series of barely connected episodes until it fizzles out when even the actors lose their patience. Some of these episodes are very funny. Volscius, for instance, gives an anguished soliloquy to his own legs in which one leg stands for love and the other for honour. The lack of structure to *The Rehearsal* serves Villiers' critical point that Baroque drama tends to lose its direction among pointlessly elaborate subplots. The play is held together by the character of Bayes with his egotism and childlike love of display: 'I'll shew you the greatest Scene that ever England saw: I mean not for words, for those I do not value; but for state, shew, and magnificence.' Bayes was one of Garrick's favourite parts (he played the role at Drury Lane almost fifty times), so *The Rehearsal* was frequently revived until Sheridan's *The Critic* superseded it in popularity.

Sheridan was not interested in classical dramatic theory. The anonymous review of the first night of *The Critic* in *The Morning Chronicle* (1 November 1779) saw the play as 'rather an act of angry retaliation than a dramatic satire, founded on general principles.' In part the satire is political rather than literary. Puff writes pro-government journalism and has written his play, 'The Spanish Armada', as a piece of nationalistic propaganda. Early audiences readily identified Lord Burleigh (who comes on to the stage, thinks deeply, shakes his head and silently leaves) with George III's puppet prime minister, Lord North, who was accused of doing nothing beyond looking grave while the American colonies asserted their independence.

While Villiers' approach is an ideological one, Sheridan is more interested in the practical craft of writing. Bayes follows a false literary ideal, Puff demonstrates how close poor and good writing are to each other. Puff's ideas are not bad but they are mishandled technically. He has difficulty in getting his characters offstage; at one point he wants his actors to exit while kneeling and at another they end up in an apparently unresolvable deadlock with daggers pointed at each other's hearts. When Puff gives dubious advice about plotting a play ('let your underplot have as little connection with your main plot as possible') or notes that 'nothing introduces you a heroine like soft music', he is showing a genuine, if misguided, knowledge of the theatre. Some celebrated plays *do* have subplots that have almost nothing to do with the main plot; heroines *are* often introduced with a lush signature tune. While Villiers disapproves of what he portrays, Sheridan cherishes his ludicrous theatrical conventions. He enjoys, for instance, the previously unspoken rule that female characters must dress in white as soon as they become insane. In a stage direction he notes that Don Whiskerandos dies in a duel 'after the usual number of wounds given', since the audience would be unaware of this comment (stage directions are not read out during a performance), this must be an in-joke about unconvincing fight scenes for the enjoyment of the cast. The exchange between Tilburina and her father, the Governor, in which she begs him to release Don Whiskerandos, reveals how close Puff comes to good writing. He conveys the urgency of the conversation by making it a terse, stichomythic exchange. Tilburina describes the rewards the Spanish would give while the Governor proclaims his loyalty to England. But Sheridan subverts Puff's rhetoric by suggesting that the Governor can be bribed if the price is right. Tragic idealism is undercut by comic realism:

Tilburina: My lover!

Governor: My country!

Tilburina: Tilburina!

Governor: England!

Tilburina: A title!

Governor: Honour!

Tilburina: A pension!

Governor: Conscience!

Tilburina: A thousand pounds!

Governor: Hah! Thou hast touched me nearly!

If *The Critic* satirises inept playwrights and absurd conventions, it is also a celebration of theatricality. As ever with Sheridan, *The Critic* contains an element of complicity with what it seems to ridicule. *The Rivals* mocked sentimentality and embraced it with Faulkland's character. *The School for Scandal* portrayed the harm done by malicious rumours and newspaper articles while enjoying the imaginative playfulness of gossip. *The Critic* lampoons the clichés of dramatic writing while also relishing their absurdity. Puff's final spectacular display of British naval power allows Sheridan both to mock strident displays of patriotism and to collude in them. Olivier conveyed the pleasure involved in such displays in a visual metaphor: while stepping upstage to orchestrate the special effects, Puff accidentally flies up into the air astride a rising piece of scenery and then swings across the stage – he is 'carried away' by his own work.

The Morning Chronicle's description of *The Critic* as an 'angry retaliation' is surprising. The humour is generally genial, leaning towards visual gags and tongue-in-cheek solemnity. Comic stereotypes are plentiful, beginning with the quarrelling Dangles, who put on a performance of marital happiness before visitors for fear of hostile gossip; as Dangle complains: 'Plague on't, now we must appear loving and affectionate, or Sneer will hitch us into a story.' The satire only becomes harsh in the treatment of Sir Fretful Plagiary. Sir Fretful is a caricature of the prolific playwright Richard Cumberland, who antagonised Sheridan with his overtly sentimental tragedies and his pro-government views. The part offers an actor an opportunity to create a brief study of self-tormenting egotism. Sir Fretful is so obsessed with his own 'greatness' as a writer that he can barely communicate with other people; he is his only subject.

Although the first act, which Sheridan thought his best piece of dramatic writing, clashes stylistically with the two following acts, the play is unified by an awareness of the pervasiveness of performance in modern society. The Dangles pretend to be happily married in public and Sir Fanciful acts out a high-minded contempt for the newspaper reviews of his plays, which he secretly reads. Puff made a living for two years by pretending to be various victims of misfortune, including 'a widow with six helpless children', and appealing for charity in the newspapers. He confesses that these confidence tricks were 'rather against my conscience', suggesting a glimmer of humanity, so he became a journalist. Sheridan's political indignation permeates Puff's breezy comments about how easy it is for the newspapers to shape public opinion: 'the number of those who go through the fatigue of judging for themselves is very small indeed!' But there is also some admiration for the audacity of the journalists and the size of the lies they print. Puff is working on a fictitious story about the assassination of the Whig leader – he plans 'to shoot CHARLES FOX in the *Morning Post*'.

Sheridan makes several jokes at his own expense. When Sir Fanciful Plagiary is asked if he sends his plays to Drury Lane, he replies that 'it is not always safe to leave a play in the hands of those who write themselves.' Presumably he fears that Sheridan would plagiarise his work. The joke is on both playwrights; Sir Fanciful's surname reveals that he is a hopelessly derivative author but Sheridan acknowledges how much his own plays owe to the Restoration Comedy of Manners. Puff also resembles his creator. Both men are playwrights and political journalists; in the period between the first performance of *The School for Scandal* and the writing of *The Critic*, Sheridan wrote journalism for the Whig newspaper *The Englishman*. Both Puff and Sheridan are intent on media manipulation (in his later years Sheridan financed journalists and papers who supported the Whigs). As the manager of Drury Lane he was also, as Puff describes himself, 'a Professor of the Art of Puffing', writing promotional copy for his own productions. Sheridan's theme is again one of complicity. He is troublingly aware of how easy it is to become the kind of people we claim to despise.

Sheridan is a particularly modern dramatist in his perception of the power of the media to refashion reality. Like *The School for Scandal*, the first line of *The Critic* makes a reference to the press. Dangle reads the titles of the articles in his newspaper out loud: '"Brutus to Lord North" – "Letter the second, on the STATE OF THE

ARMY."' Brutus is one of the classical pseudonyms used by eighteenth-century political commentators; the most famous of these authors, Junius, was a strong literary and political influence on the young Sheridan during his years at Bath. The first act of *The Critic* conveys the amount of power such self-appointed 'experts' wield. Dangle emphasises the arbitrariness of political authority by dismissing his wife's views: 'What has a woman to do with politics, Mrs Dangle?' Anonymous authors using classical pseudonyms deserve to be taken seriously but women do not. Later, Puff claims that he determines government promotions through his journalism. Rather than reporting the news, he creates it and even helps to form the government that pays him for his loyalty. He can 'with the carelessness of a casual paragraph suggest officers into commands – to which they have no pretensions but their wishes.' Sheridan indicates how governments would increasingly be tempted to make decisions according to what plays well to journalists and political pundits.

The Critic is equally astute about our society's unending need for entertainment. Although Tynan asserted that the 'single theme' of the play was the 'undressing [of] the eighteenth-century tragic muse', many of Puff's theatrical strategies are easily translatable into the conventions of the Hollywood blockbuster. The idea in 'The Spanish Armada' of foregrounding a love affair between two people divided by antagonistic cultures against a spectacular historical event also became box-office gold in James Cameron's *Titanic* (1997). The play's revelations of unsuspected family connections between different characters (Justice: I am thy father, here's thy mother, there/Thy uncle – this thy first cousin, and those/Are all your near relations!) anticipates the revelations about Luke Skywalker's father and sister in the original *Star Wars* trilogy (1977-1983). Puff claims that 'I don't attempt to strike out anything new – but I take it I improve on the established modes.' He exploits dramatic formulas that are still being used in the film industry. The genial humour of *The Critic* invites the audience to succumb to the absurd plot devices of 'The Spanish Armada' but Puff's praise of his own work warns us of the price to be paid: 'Now, gentlemen, this scene goes entirely for what we call SITUATION and STAGE EFFECT, by which the greatest applause may be obtained, without the assistance of language, sentiment or character: pray mark!' Ultimately his play attempts to do without the elements which make the theatre thought-provoking such as language and character conflict. He wants to create a patriotic and emotive spectacle, which compels the audience to applaud but not to think. The importance of words is signalled by Sheridan in the death of Don Whiskerandos (which parodies Hotspur's interrupted dying speech in Shakespeare's *Henry IV, Part One*) when the Beefeater gives equal attention to the hero's mortality and his syntax: 'stern death/Cut short his being, and the noun at once.' The final words of the play, belong to Puff who addresses his actors: 'Well, pretty well – but not quite perfect – so ladies and gentlemen, if you please, we'll rehearse this piece again tomorrow.' The structure of *The Critic* is cyclical. Tomorrow will be the same as today: the same mixture of clichéd entertainment and jingoism will be purveyed to a compliant public.

The playwright Charles Dibdin in his *The Musical Tour of Mr Dibdin* (1788) complained that the satire in *The Critic* was so effective that it prevented the writing of new tragedies. He issued a challenge: 'I defy Mr Sheridan himself to write a tragedy so as to steer clear of his own lash'. In 1799, almost twenty years after *The Critic*, Sheridan wrote *Pizarro*. Since this tragedy is little known, an outline of the plot will emphasise how much the play differs in subject matter and style from his previous works. The events are loosely based around the sixteenth-century conquest of Peru. Pizarro is leading a Spanish army intent on invading the country. He means to marry the daughter of the Peruvian King to legitimise his rule but the invasion is failing. This is partly due to the Peruvian resistance, led by Rolla, but also to a dispute among the Spaniards about the reason for their presence in the new world. While Pizarro pursues military victory, his mistress Elvira and the priest Las Casas argue for a peaceful approach involving education and an improved cultivation of the land. Alonzo, disgusted by Pizarro's ruthlessness, has deserted and joined the Peruvians. These events have an impact on the romantic lives of all the major characters. Among the Peruvians Alonzo marries Cora and has a baby with her; Cora had previously been engaged to Rolla. Equally, Pizarro and Elvira are disillusioned with each other. When Alonzo is captured during battle, Rolla switches places with him in prison. Elvira persuades Rolla to assassinate Pizarro and leads him to their tent. Rolla refuses to murder the sleeping Spanish leader and wakes him. Pizarro is impressed by Rolla's nobility, offers him safe passage out of the camp and also orders Elvira's execution. Two Spanish soldiers arrive with Cora's stolen baby. Rolla snatches the child and escapes under gunfire. Wounded, he returns the baby to Cora and dies in Alonzo's arms. The Spanish army follows only to lose a final battle. Pizarro challenges Alonzo to single combat and almost kills the younger man before he freezes on seeing Elvira dressed as a novice nun. (In Spain, Pizarro had abducted the willing Elvira from a nunnery and killed her brother.) Alonzo stabs the guilt-stricken Pizarro and the defeated Spaniards swear that they will leave Peru.

Arnold Hare calls the play 'A semi-operatic spectacular'. The action is often accompanied by music and songs. Sheridan carefully choreographed the temple scene in Act Two. The stage directions give some idea of the grandeur of his conception: 'The Temple of the Sun: it represents the magnificence of Peruvian idolatry: in the centre is the altar. – A solemn march. – The Warriors and King enter on one side of the Temple.' Equally, Rolla's escape with Cora's baby in the last act across 'a Torrent falling down the Precipice, over which a Bridge is formed by a fell'd tree' caused a sensation. (Sir Thomas Lawrence's painting of John Philip Kemble as Rolla with the baby became an iconic Romantic image.)

The overwhelming financial success of *Pizarro* gave it the nickname 'the Gold Mines of Peru' but the critics questioned the overblown quality of the writing. Thomas Moore complains in his biography of Sheridan that 'it is the dialogue of this play that is unworthy of its author, and ought never, from either motives of profit or the vanity of success, to have been coupled with his name. The style in which it is written belongs neither to verse or prose, but is a sort of amphibious native of both'. John Loftis' *Sheridan and the Drama of Georgian England* (1976) makes a similar point while emphasising *Pizarro*'s political content: 'Even the best orations of politicians make dull reading in later time, and too much of *Pizarro* sounds like political debate.' David Francis Taylor disputes the negative views of the play's rhetoric. He argues in *Theatres of Opposition* (2012) that Sheridan deliberately demonstrates 'the inability of eloquence, however applauded, to counter regimes of despotism and torture.' Taylor places *Pizarro* against the atrocities which occurred during the Irish Rebellion of 1798: 'The Irish playwright provides his audience with a narrative that not only critiques the bloody British suppression of Ireland, a catastrophe which took the lives of 20,000-30,000 people, but also points to the tragic failure of oppositionist rhetoric to prevent this or any imperial horror.'

Taylor's argument is compelling but it ignores the pervasive bathos in the play. Pizarro's frequent quarrels with Elvira suggest the play's vulnerability to laughter:

Elvira: Why should I retire?
Pizarro: Because men are to meet here, and on manly business.
Elvira: O, men! men!

This clumsy dialogue could have been uttered by Tilburina and her father in 'The Spanish Armada'. (*Pizarro* seems to take seriously the tragic clichés which *The Critic* had ridiculed.) But Sheridan's early audiences admired this exchange. They recognised that Elvira is not simply Pizarro's mistress. She refuses to be intimidated by him or any other masculine authority. The passage emphasises the gender politics of the play. The Spanish invaders are defined by their machismo while Cora and Elvira, although contrasted as the stereotypical 'good mother' and 'fallen woman', both stand for peace.

Sheridan's drastic change of style in the twenty years between *The Critic* and *Pizarro* was influenced by important changes in the theatre during the late eighteenth century. With the increasing population of London came a growing demand for mass entertainment. When Drury Lane closed in 1791, Sheridan rebuilt it to house almost twice as many people. In 1779, when *The Critic* was staged, a capacity audience consisted of 2000 people. When the theatre reopened in 1794 it could contain over 3600 people. Robert Southey gives an account of the impact of the new Drury Lane in his *Letters from England* (1807):

> I had heard much of this theatre, and was prepared for wonder; still the size, the height, the beauty, the splendour, astonished me. Imagine a pit capable of holding a thousand persons, four tiers of boxes supported by pillars scarcely thicker than a man's arm, and two galleries in front, the higher one at such a distance, that they who are in it must be content to see the show, without hoping to hear the dialogue; the colours blue and silver, and the whole illuminated with chandeliers of cut glass, not partially nor parsimoniously; every part as distinctly seen as if in the noon sunshine. After the first feeling of surprise and delight, I began to wish that a massier style of architecture had been adopted. The pillars, which are iron, are so slender as to give an idea of insecurity; their lightness is much

admired, but it is disproportionate and out of place. There is a row of private boxes on each side of the pit, on a level with it; convenient they must doubtless be to those who occupy them, and profitable to the proprietors of the house; but they deform the theatre.

The people in the galleries were very noisy before the representation began, whistling and calling to the musicians; and they amused themselves by throwing orange-peel into the pit and upon the stage: after the curtain drew up they were sufficiently silent. The pit was soon filled; the lower side-boxes did not begin to fill till towards the middle of the first act, because that part of the audience is too fashionable to come in time; the back part of the front boxes not till the half play; they were then filled with a swarm of prostitutes, and of men who came to meet them. In the course of the evening there were two or three quarrels there which disturbed the performance, and perhaps ended in duels the next morning.

The actors found the scale and acoustics of the new Drury Lane intimidating. In such a huge space the subtle gestures which had characterised Sheridan's comedies were easily lost. Even Sarah Siddons, who excelled in intense tragic roles, looked out at the vast auditorium and declared that she would never have been able to establish her reputation in such a 'wilderness'. The new theatre demanded a style of acting based on emphatic gestures and a powerful projection of the voice. It also encouraged the vogue for spectacular visual effects.

By the 1790s the cultural balance of Europe had shifted. When Sheridan wrote his comedies in the 1770s, Paris was the home of the Arts. An English playwright would look to Molière, Racine and Marivaux. During the French Revolution, beginning in 1789, the British theatre turned to Germany for its inspiration. Sheridan was two years younger than the major German poet and playwright Johann Wolfgang von Goethe. Both men were influenced by the works of Oliver Goldsmith and had their first plays staged in their mid-twenties. Goethe was a prominent member of the *Sturm und Drang* (Storm and Stress) movement, which prioritised passion over wit and elegance. By the 1790s the new German playwrights were frequently imitated and translated by English authors. New plays by August Friedrich Ferdinand von Kotzebue enjoyed a particular vogue. In March 1798 Drury Lane staged Benjamin Thompson's *The Stranger*, based on Kotzebue's *Menschenhass und Reue*. Sheridan revised Thompson's text and the play had a good run. Later in the same year Elizabeth Inchbald adapted Kotzebue's *Das Kind der Liebe* as *Lovers' Vows* for Covent Garden. Inchbald's play is now chiefly remembered because it is used for the amateur theatricals in Jane Austen's *Mansfield Park* (1814) but it made Kotzebue into a hot property as Paul Baines and Edward Burns explain in their introduction to *Five Romantic Plays, 1768-1821* (2000):

> *Lovers' Vows* was first performed at Covent Garden on Thursday 11 October 1798, and was an immediate hit; altogether it ran for forty-two nights in the season, making it by some distance Covent Garden's most successful venture that season. The royal family went to see it on 24 October.

Sheridan based *Pizarro* on a free translation of Kotzebue's *The Spanish in Peru*. Beyond his awareness of the play's box-office potential, he was interested in Kotzebue's political message. *Lovers' Vows* caused controversy in England over its dismissive attitude to social class. (In 1819 Kotzebue was assassinated by a German Nationalist.) Sheridan's cynical declaration that 'Kotzebue and German sausages are the order of the day', concealed his determination to use the skeleton of *The Spanish in Peru* to build a politically contemporary play. William Pitt the Younger claimed after seeing *Pizarro* that 'there's nothing new in it, for I heard it long ago at Hastings' trial.' The play freely borrows from Sheridan's parliamentary rhetoric. Rolla's sarcastic description of the protection offer by Pizarro's Spanish army is derived from an image Sheridan used to describe how the British exploited India while claiming to protect it: 'such protection as vultures give to lambs – covering and devouring them!' Some audience members saw Pizarro as a portrait of Napoleon and applauded the play as a gesture of defiance against the French threat of invasion. But *Pizarro* was also a critique of British colonialism. As Arnold Hare claims 'There were topical and political overtones that the audience of the day were not slow to pick up; the 'noble savage' element and the humanitarian sympathies of the play had a clear relationship to the current debate on the slave trade, and brought William Wilberforce to the theatre for the first time in twenty years.' In reviewing the opening performance on 24 May 1799, the *Morning Post* of the following day praised the play for depicting 'the energies of a free, brave, and generous people, fighting for liberty against oppression.'

Sheridan wanted for most of his creative life to write a drama about characters living in the wilds. In his early twenties he produced an untitled dramatic fragment in which a group of outlaws disguise themselves as demons to frighten their enemies. Through the 1780s and 1790s he boasted that his previous plays would be eclipsed when he finished a musical drama called *The Foresters*. These fragments and intentions reveal a generally ignored side of Sheridan, which responded to the Gothic movement and early Romanticism. His idea of portraying sinister but noble outlaws in a forest setting anticipates Schiller's famous *Sturm und Drang* play *The Robbers* (1781). With *Pizarro* Sheridan created his drama of life in a primal woodland: 'A Bank covered by a wild Wood and Rocks – Cora, sitting on the root of a tree, is playing with her Child'. Sheridan's evocation of 'noble savages' resisting the invasion of a corrupt civilisation recalls Jean-Jacques Rousseau's political and educational views. Elvira repeats the author's anti-colonial message in the final speech: 'Spaniards returning to your native home assure your rulers, they mistake the road to power. – Tell them, that the pursuits of avarice, conquest and ambition, never yet made a people happy, or a nation great.'

When Kemble was congratulated for his performance as Rolla, he advised his admirers to 'Carry your wonder to Mrs Siddons; she has made a heroine of a soldier's trull.' Elvira is Pizarro's mistress and Kotzebue's original play emphasised her sexuality by having her also attempt to seduce Alonzo. Sheridan and Siddons however created a study of moral regeneration. By ultimately donning the robes of her noviciate she regains her radical innocence. It is the vision of the redeemed Elvira which defeats Pizarro rather than Alonzo's sword. In contrast Pizarro cannot change. Alonzo declares of his enemy 'Thou still wilt live, and still wilt be – Pizarro.' But in his confrontation with Rolla, Pizarro recognises that his implacable nature is a self-created prison. He closes the fourth act with the wish that he could escape his own constrictive identity: 'I would I cou'd retrace my steps – I cannot – Would I could evade my own reflections! – No! – thought and memory are my Hell.'

Pizarro is an historically important Romantic play about liberty and intended genocide (The Spaniard Davilla cries out 'Death to the whole Peruvian race!'). It is also a melodrama, signalling the decline of Sheridan's literary talent and the beginning of a long period of mediocre writing in the British theatre. Perhaps it is appropriate that a book about such an elusive figure as Sheridan should end on an ambivalent note but this is an unjust response to his three greatest comedies. During the temple scene in *Pizarro*, according to the stage directions, 'Fire from above lights upon the Altar.' What better symbol could there be for Sheridan's erratic but dazzling career?

Bibliography

The Plays

The Rivals, ed. Tiffany Stern (New Mermaids, 2004).

The Rivals, ed. Susan Macklin with a personal essay by Michael Billington (Longman, 1985).

The School for Scandal, ed. Ann Blake (New Mermaids, 2004).

The Critic, ed. David Crane (New Mermaids, 1989).

Plays, ed. Cecil Price (Oxford University Press, 1975).

The School for Scandal *and Other Plays*, ed. Michael Cordner (Oxford University Press, 1998).

Recordings

The Rivals, directed by Rachel Kavanagh, Heritage Theatre, 2004.

The School for Scandal, with Edith Evans, Naxos cd, recorded 1956.

The School for Scandal, directed by Nick Havinga and Michael Langham, Broadway Classics, 1975.

The School for Scandal, directed by Elizabeth Freestone, Stage on Screen, 2010.

Anthologies and Other Plays

Paul Baines and Edward Burns (eds.), *Five Romantic Plays*, 1768-1821 (Oxford University Press, 2000).

Melinda C. Finberg (ed.), *Eighteenth-Century Women Dramatists* (Oxford University Press, 2001).

David W. Lindsay (ed.), The Beggar's Opera *and Other Eighteenth-Century Plays* (1928; Everyman, 1995).

Scott McMillan (ed.), *Restoration and Eighteenth-Century Comedy* (Norton, 1997).

John Vanbrugh, The Relapse *and Other Plays*, ed. Brean Hammond (Oxford University Press, 2004).

David Womersley (ed.), *Restoration Drama: An Anthology* (Blackwell, 2000).

Criticism and Biography

Peter Davison (ed.), *Sheridan: Comedies* (Palgrave, 1986).

Arnold Hare, *Richard Brinsley Sheridan*, Writers and their Work series (Profile Books, 1981).

Linda Kelly, *Richard Brinsley Sheridan: A Life* (1997; Faber, 2008).

John Loftis, *Sheridan and the Drama of Georgian England* (Basil Blackwell, 1976).

Thomas Moore, *Memoirs of the Life of the Rt. Hon. Richard Brinsley Sheridan*, in two volumes (1825; Books for Libraries Press, 1971).

James Morwood and David Crane (eds.), *Sheridan Studies* (Cambridge University Press, 1995).

Margaret Oliphant, *Sheridan* (1883; Cambridge University Press, 2011).

Fintan O'Toole, *A Traitor's Kiss* (Granta, 1997).

Paul Ranger, *The School for Scandal* (Macmillan, 1986).

David Francis Taylor, *Theatres of Opposition* (Oxford University Press, 2012).

Katharine Worth, *Sheridan and Goldsmith* (Macmillan, 1992).

Background Reading

Robyn Asleson (ed.), *A Passion for Performance: Sarah Siddons and her Portraitists* (J. Paul Getty Museum, 1999).

Matthew Bevis, *Comedy: A Very Short Introduction* (Oxford, 2013).

Paula Byrne, *Perdita: The Life of Mary Robinson* (Harper Collins, 2004).

Elizabeth Eger, *Bluestockings* (Palgrave Macmillan, 2010).

Amanda Foreman, *Georgiana, Duchess of Devonshire* (Harper Collins, 1998).

William Hague, *William Pitt the Younger* (Harper Collins, 2004).

Ian Kelly, *Beau Brummell, the Ultimate Dandy* (Hodder, 2005).

Ian Kelly, *Mr Foote's Other Leg* (Picador, 2012).

Andy Merriman, *Margaret Rutherford: Dreadnought with Good Manners* (Aurum, 2009).

A.M. Nagler, *A Source Book in Theatrical History* (1952; Dover, 1959).

Jesse Norman, *Edmund Burke, Philosopher, Politician, Prophet* (William Collins, 2013).

Robert Southey, *Letters from England* (1807; Alan Sutton, 1984).

Claire Tomalin, *Mrs Jordan's Profession* (Penguin, 1994).

Robert Whelan, *The Other National Theatre* (Jacob Tonson, 2013).

T.H. White, *The Age of Scandal* (Jonathan Cape, 1950).

GREENWICH EXCHANGE BOOKS

STUDENT GUIDE LITERARY SERIES

The Greenwich Exchange Student Guide Literary Series is a collection of essays on major or contemporary serious writers in English and selected European languages. The series is for the student, the teacher and the 'common reader' and is an ideal resource for libraries. The *Times Educational Supplement* praised these books, saying, "The style of [this series] has a pressure of meaning behind it. Readers should learn from that ... If art is about selection, perception and taste, then this is it."

The series includes:

Antonin Artaud by Lee Jamieson (978-1-871551-98-3)
W.H. Auden by Stephen Wade (978-1-871551-36-5)
Jane Austen by Pat Levy (978-1-871551-89-1)
Honoré de Balzac by Wendy Mercer (978-1-871551-48-8)
Louis de Bernières by Rob Spence (978-1-906075-13-2)
William Blake by Peter Davies (978-1-871551-27-3)
The Brontës by Peter Davies (978-1-871551-24-2)
Robert Browning by John Lucas (978-1-871551-59-4)
Lord Byron by Andrew Keanie (978-1-871551-83-9)
Samuel Taylor Coleridge by Andrew Keanie (978-1-871551-64-8)
Joseph Conrad by Martin Seymour-Smith (978-1-871551-18-1)
William Cowper by Michael Thorn (978-1-871551-25-9)
Charles Dickens by Robert Giddings (987-1-871551-26-6)
Emily Dickinson by Marnie Pomeroy (978-1-871551-68-6)
John Donne by Sean Haldane (978-1-871551-23-5)
Elizabethan Love Poets by John Greening (978-1-906075-52-1)
Ford Madox Ford by Anthony Fowles (978-1-871551-63-1)
Sigmund Freud by Stephen Wilson (978-1-906075-30-9)
The Stagecraft of Brian Friel by David Grant (978-1-871551-74-7)
Robert Frost by Warren Hope (978-1-871551-70-9)
Patrick Hamilton by John Harding (978-1-871551-99-0)
Thomas Hardy by Sean Haldane (978-1-871551-33-4)
Seamus Heaney by Warren Hope (978-1-871551-37-2)
Joseph Heller by Anthony Fowles (978-1-871551-84-6)
George Herbert By Neil Curry and Natasha Curry (978-1-906075-40-8)
Gerard Manley Hopkins by Sean Sheehan (978-1-871551-77-8)
James Joyce by Michael Murphy (978-1-871551-73-0)
Philip Larkin by Warren Hope (978-1-871551-35-8)

Laughter in the Dark – The Plays of Joe Orton by Arthur Burke
  (978-1-871551-56-3)
George Orwell by Warren Hope (978-1-871551-42-6)
Sylvia Plath by Marnie Pomeroy (978-1-871551-88-4)
Poets of the First World War by John Greening (978-1-871551-79-2)
Alexander Pope by Neil Curry (978-1-906075-23-1)
Marcel Proust by Derwent May (978-1-906075-76-7)
Restoration Drama by Sean Elliott (978-1-906075-79-8)
Philip Roth by Paul McDonald (978-1-871551-72-3)
Shakespeare's *A Midsummer Night's Dream* by Matt Simpson
  (978-1-871551-90-7)
Shakespeare's *As You Like It* by Matt Simpson (978-1-906075-46-0)
Shakespeare's *Hamlet* by Peter Davies (978-1-906075-12-5)
Shakespeare's *Julius Caesar* by Matt Simpson (978-1-906075-37-8)
Shakespeare's *King Lear* by Peter Davies (978-1-871551-95-2)
Shakespeare's *Macbeth* by Matt Simpson (978-1-871551-69-3)
Shakespeare's *The Merchant of Venice* by Alan Ablewhite
  (978-1-871551-96-9)
Shakespeare's *Much Ado about Nothing* by Matt Simpson
  (978-1-906075-01-9)
Shakespeare's Non-Dramatic Poetry by Martin Seymour-Smith
  (978-1-871551-22-8)
Shakespeare's *Othello* by Matt Simpson (978-1-871551-71-6)
Shakespeare's *Romeo and Juliet* by Matt Simpson (978-1-906075-17-0)
Shakespeare's Second Tetralogy: *Richard II–Henry V*
  by John Lucas (978-1-871551-97-6)
Shakespeare's Sonnets by Martin Seymour-Smith (978-1-871551-38-9)
Shakespeare's *The Tempest* by Matt Simpson (978-1-871551-75-4)
Shakespeare's *Twelfth Night* by Matt Simpson (978-1-871551-86-0)
Shakespeare's *The Winter's Tale* by John Lucas (978-1-871551-80-8)
Percy Bysshe Shelley by Andrew Keanie (978-1-871551-59-0)
Tobias Smollett by Robert Giddings (978-1-871551-21-1)
Alfred, Lord Tennyson by Michael Thorn (978-1-871551-20-4)
Dylan Thomas by Peter Davies (978-1-871551-78-5)
William Wordsworth by Andrew Keanie (978-1-871551-57-0)
W.B. Yeats by John Greening (978-1-871551-34-1)

FOCUS ON SERIES

(ISBN prefix 978-1-906075 applies to all the following titles):

Jane Austen: *Mansfield Park* by Anthony Fowles (61-3)
James Baldwin: *Go Tell It on the Mountain* by Neil Root (44-6)
William Blake: *Songs of Innocence and Experience* by Matt Simpson (26-2)
Charlotte Brontë: *Jane Eyre* by Philip McCarthy (60-6)
Emily Brontë: *Wuthering Heights* by Matt Simpson (10-1)
Truman Capote: *Breakfast at Tiffany's* by Neil Root (53-8)
Angela Carter: *The Bloody Chamber and Other Stories* by Angela Topping (25-5)
The Poetry of John Clare by Angela Topping (48-4)
George Eliot: *Middlemarch* by John Axon (06-4)
T.S. Eliot: *The Waste Land* by Matt Simpson (09-5)
F. Scott Fitzgerald: *The Great Gatsby* by Peter Davies (29-3)
Michael Frayn: *Spies* by Angela Topping (08-8)
The Poetry of Robert Graves by Michael Cullup (60-9)
Thomas Hardy: *Poems of 1912–13* by John Greening (04-0)
Thomas Hardy: *Tess of the D'Urbervilles* by Philip McCarthy (45-3)
The Poetry of Tony Harrison by Scan Sheehan (15-6)
The Poetry of Ted Hughes by John Greening (05-7)
Aldous Huxley: *Brave New World* by Neil Root (41-5)
James Joyce: *A Portrait of the Artist as a Young Man* by Matt Simpson (07-1)
John Keats: *Isabella; or, the Pot of Basil, The Eve of St Agnes, Lamia* and *La Belle Dame sans Merci* by Andrew Keanie (27-9)
The Poetry of Mary Leapor by Stephen Van-Hagen (35-4)
V.S. Naipaul: *A Bend in the River* by John Harding (74-3)
Harold Pinter by Lee Jamieson (16-3)
Jean Rhys: *Wide Sargasso Sea* by Anthony Fowles (34-7)
The Poetry of Jonathan Swift by Stephen Van-Hagen (57-6)
Edward Thomas by John Greening (28-6)
Wordsworth and Coleridge: *Lyrical Ballads* (1798) by Andrew Keanie (20-0)

Other subjects covered by Greenwich Exchange books:
Biography
Education
Philosophy